CASEY STENGEL

BASEBALL'S
'OLD PROFESSOR'

CASEY STENGEL

BASEBALL'S
'OLD PROFESSOR'

DAVID CATANEO

Cumberland House
Nashville, Tennessee

Published by
    Cumberland House Publishing, Inc.
    431 Harding Industrial Drive
    Nashville, TN 37211-3160

Cover design: Gore Studio, Inc.
Text design: John Mitchell

Library of Congress Cataloging-in-Publication Data
Cataneo, David.
  Casey Stengel : baseball's 'old professor' / David Cataneo.
      p. cm.
Includes bibliographical references and index.
  ISBN 1-58182-327-4 (pbk. : alk. paper)
  1. Stengel, Casey. 2. Baseball managers—United States—Biography.
I. Title.

GV865.S8C38 2003
796.357'092—dc21

                                                        2003002392

Printed in Canada
1 2 3 4 5 6 7—09 08 07 06 05 04 03

CONTENTS

To M. E. and Skippy

ACKNOWLEDGMENTS

Thank you to all who took the time to reach back once more and recall Casey:

Maury Allen, Rugger Ardizoia, Hank Bauer, Ray Berres, Bobby Brown, Tommy Byrne, Galen Cisco, Will Cloney, Jerry Coleman, Rod Dedeaux, Mel Duezabou, Darrell Evans, Eleanor Evans, Mark Freeman, Tom Ferguson, Tommy Holmes, Tim Horgan, Ralph Houk, Ron Hunt, Al Jackson, Art Johnson, Eddie Joost, Rod Kanehl, Clif Keane, Jack Lang, Dario Lodigiani, Al Lopez, Harry Minor, Bill Raimondi, Bobby Richardson, Bob Sales, Sibby Sisti, Moose Skowron, Chuck Stevens, George Sullivan, Sam Suplizio, Ron Swoboda, Chuck Symonds, Max West, and Wally Westlake.

Extra special gratitude to Bob Case.

Thanks also to Dick Beverage and Patty Helmsworth of the Association of Professional Ball Players of America, Dick Johnson of the Boston Sports Museum, Jim Gallagher of the Boston University College of Communication library, Stephen Grabowski of the *Boston Herald*, Tim Wiles of the National Baseball Hall of Fame library, Jennifer L. Jones, Emily Petunia Cataneo, Carlos Smith, Palourdes Cataneo, Will Lenharth, and Christine McIntyre.

And thank you, Ron Pitkin and John Mitchell of Cumberland House, for dispensing opportunity, support, and patience.

INTRODUCTION

R od Kanehl, the original Met, was just wondering. "Why a book about Casey?" he asked. "You know, a lot of people these days never even heard of Casey Stengel."

Well, yeah. Exactly.

And a lot of people nowadays have never heard of George C. Marshall, Enrico Fermi, H. L. Mencken, Artie Shaw, or the Treaty of Versailles, because none of these appear regularly on MTV.

People nowadays have forgotten a lot worth remembering. In this book, we only have room to examine Casey.

I confess to having a longtime fascination with Stengel. I have always enjoyed talking about him, reading about him, writing about him.

It wasn't because of all those World Series champi-onships—the Yankees dynasty was just one more great thing that ended right after I was born.

It wasn't because of any poignant firsthand experi-ences. I never covered Casey as a newspaper reporter. I never saw him manage a game, not even on television. I did see him once or twice at Yankee Stadium Old-Timers Days, but it was hardly a searing image—pinstriped jersey Number 37 hanging on a bony back. I did meet him once, when I was a teenager, for about two seconds. I got an autograph. He gave me his famous how-are-you-kid stage wink. And he was drunk.

Still, I jumped at the chance to write a book about him, and not just because I'm getting third notices from the phone company. The reason is simple.

In the annals of baseball, of all the dearly departed characters who have scraped through dugouts and scratched at flannel, who would have been most fun to take out for a beer or three?

That's a no-brainer. Pull up a stool and a swizzle stick for Casey Stengel.

Who would have been more fascinating? Babe Ruth? Think of the belching. Mickey Mantle? Think of the slurring. Ted Williams? Not bad, but you'd have needed earplugs. Joe DiMaggio? Perfect, if you like long silences, as in year-long silences. And he'd have made you pick up the tab.

I'll take Stengel. He would blow cigarette smoke in your face, order two at a time, and spew great stories until light crept around the window shades.

"If you love baseball, you love Casey," said Bob Case, Stengel's friend and business manager. "Baseball was his love. He loved the old days. He loved to talk about them. (John) McGraw and all those guys. Funny things. They had a clubhouse in Boston and there was a floor under it, and they would hide guys under it to listen to the other managers. About a tour of Cuba where they were paid in gold bullion. About a trip to China with McGraw."

Except for a few nooks and crannies, Stengel could cover everything in baseball, from Ty Cobb to Andy Messersmith. Nobody else played for McGraw at the Polo Grounds and managed Choo Choo Coleman at the Polo Grounds. Not many have firsthand mentions in *The Glory of Their Times* and *Ball Four*.

Think of it. Stengel was born in 1890, when Abner Doubleday was still sitting around ruminating on Antietam. He died in 1975, when Derek Jeter was in the sandbox, making the baby girls crazy.

Outfielder Stengel threw left, batted left, and thought left for the Brooklyn Dodgers, the Pittsburgh Pirates, the Philadelphia Phillies, the New York Giants, and the Boston Braves. He managed the Toledo Mud Hens, the Kansas City Blues, the minor-league Milwaukee Brewers, the Oakland Oaks, Brooklyn, the Braves (also known at the time as the Bees), the Yankees, and the Mets.

He was once the president, general manager, and manager of the team in Worcester, Massachusetts. In order to accept a job offer from Toledo, he fired himself as manager and general manager, then resigned as president.

In the same lifetime, he batted against lefty pitcher Babe Ruth and tutored lefty pitcher Tug McGraw. He shook hands with King George V, President John F. Kennedy, and comedian Buddy Hackett. He tormented Uncle Wilbert Robinson, who caught for the 1892 Baltimore Orioles, and Chris Cannizzaro, who caught for the 1974 San Diego Padres.

He was a unique character. He was nearly killed when

he was run over by a cab in Boston's Kenmore Square in 1943. He suffered a broken leg. His friends sent him get-well cards care of the psychiatric ward. He was actually convalescing in the maternity ward.

In the same lifetime, his antics were chronicled by Ring Lardner, Damon Runyon, George Bernard Shaw (he covered an American baseball exhibition in London), Jimmy Breslin, and Howard Cosell. He played at Brooklyn's Ebbets Field the year it opened. He managed in the Houston Astrodome the year it opened.

Just imagine the stories.

In the course of writing this book, I worked hard to try to avoid talking to the usual suspects about Stengel. There have been many fine volumes written about him, including top works by Maury Allen, Robert W. Creamer, and Ira Berkow and Jim Kaplan. So I tried to find as many guys as I could who weren't nicknamed Whitey or Yogi. And it worked, because the batboys and backups all had great Casey stories, too.

Everybody has great Casey stories.

Do you think stories about Stengel—a guy who was born two months before Dwight Eisenhower, a guy who was really old when Elvis was really young—are irrelevant in these edgy, hip, youth-oriented times?

Not if you like baseball. In baseball, the past—not to be confused with nostalgia—is a big part of the fun. The past is never past anyhow.

Pick a very twenty-first century name.

Barry Bonds.

He played for Dusty Baker who played for Eddie Mathews who played for Charlie Grimm who warmed the same dugout bench with Casey Stengel on the 1919 Pittsburgh Pirates.

Ichiro Suzuki.

He played for Lou Piniella who played for Billy Martin who played for Casey Stengel, who was almost like a father to him.

See? So 113 years after his birth, seventy-eight years after he played his final inning, thirty-eight years after he managed his final game, twenty-eight years after his death, stories of Casey Stengel, the Old Professor, are as current as an episode of *Jackass*.

Well, maybe not. But they are way more enlightening and intelligent, and at least as funny.

CASEY STENGEL

BASEBALL'S
'OLD PROFESSOR'

1

━━◆━━

THE OLD PROFESSOR

There is a story. I don't know if it's true or not. When he started with the Mets, he got everybody out there. He leaned over and he picked up a baseball and he said, "Fellows, I'm going to start at the beginning. This is a baseball."

— Mets outfielder Ron Swoboda

Charles Dillon Stengel was nicknamed "Dutch," "Casey," and the "Old Professor." Dutch because of his German ancestry; Casey because he was from Kansas City; and the Old Professor because 1) he was old, and 2) he was always exploring, examining, dissecting, discussing, and teaching baseball.

Besides the numerous advanced degrees he earned through life experience, Casey had the number-one qualification to be a great teacher:

Passion.

For people. For stories. For instruction.

For his subject matter.

Think back to your favorite teachers. They were the

3

ones who enthused over isosceles trapezoids, palpitated over dangling participles, bubbled about the Crimean War, and would talk anywhere, anytime, for as long as you could stand it, about symbolism in *The Old Man and the Sea*.

That was Stengel and baseball. He was head over heels about the game, perhaps more than anybody else, ever. He wanted to know everything about it. And he wanted to shout, in a whiskey-and-cigarette voice, what he knew to the world.

"Baseball was his life, man," said Ron Hunt, who got his uniform dirty, got hit by pitches and thus pleased Stengel mightily with the New York Mets. "*When* did he start in the game of baseball? And when he was done, he was *how old*? That's a pretty good damn string, man."

Stengel loved baseball's complexity. He loved its simplicity. He loved the enormous fun of it. He loved to talk about it, endlessly, into the night. He understood it deeply. Robert W. Creamer, one of Casey's biographers, noted that Stengel "always saw a lot of things in baseball that others didn't."

"He hated these Old-Timers Games," said Bob Sales, who covered Stengel's Mets for the old *New York Herald Tribune*. "He wouldn't have anything to do with them. He said, 'Now they can't wipe their asses with their gloves, and I want to remember them the way they were when they could play.'"

He loved baseball. And he spent a lifetime trying to get others to see it his way.

⎯⎯⎯◆⎯⎯⎯

Rod Dedeaux, *legendary University of Southern California baseball coach, grew up in the Los Angeles area in the 1920s:*

Casey was my mentor when I was in high school. Casey lived in Glendale. There was a large playground that was very active in those days called Griffith Park. It's still there. Casey would come out during the wintertime. I think he was managing Toledo in those days—the Toledo Mud Hens—and he'd come out to the ballpark. My friends and I, we'd be out there playing baseball and all kind of games every day. Casey would work us out. Hit us ground balls. Hit us pop flies. Talk baseball.

We'd all sit at his feet, as if he were Aristotle. It was so typical of him, that he loved to work out kids and teach. He was the wise man. We just worshipped him, because he was such a fountain of knowledge about baseball.

And he worked with us to try to perfect it. He had the ability to sell his ideas. And he had so many stories to tell to illustrate what he was talking about.

He liked best to teach baseball. That's why they call him the Old Professor. Teach baseball. That's what he liked.

Years later, when he was with the Yankees, I would visit with him all the time when he was back here during the winter.

He and his wife, Edna, found and recommended the house that we purchased and now live in. It's only half a mile from their house. I would go over there regularly and sit down with him, maybe spend all day long, through lunch—Edna would feed us—and we'd talk baseball. He was my mentor.

MAX WEST, *later an outfielder with Stengel's Boston Braves, also grew up in Southern California:*

I knew him long before he went to Boston. He lived in Glendale, and he was being paid to not manage Brooklyn at the time. I met him when I was a junior in high school.

He would come around to the parks. He used to like to get together young players and take them over to Griffith Park, which is by where Dodger Stadium is now. He had balls and bats. He'd hit balls to us and throw, and we'd throw.

That's all he did or talked about—baseball—all his life.

He became a good friend of my dad's. I was almost his adopted son before we got through. He and his wife had a huge home over in Glendale. Babe Herman lived near him; they were good friends. He would invite me over there, and he would just want to talk baseball.

※

WALLY WESTLAKE, *a major-league outfielder with the Pittsburgh Pirates, Saint Louis Cardinals, and others, 1947–56. He played under Stengel on the Pacific Coast League Oakland Oaks in 1946:*

Old Casey saved my butt.

I had played for the old Oakland Acorns in 1942. I was twenty-one. Then I was in the service for three years. When I returned to Oakland in '46, I had been away three years. Casey had become the manager of Oakland.

The Lord had given me some tools, but I didn't know what baseball was about. I thought I did, but I didn't. Old Casey took me under his wing. After a while, I realized you just had to sit back and listen to what he was saying. It might sound a little crazy, but he was telling you something.

He taught me how to play the outfield and play it right, how to run the bases. He taught me so damn many things.

Then he sold me to the Pirates.

The next year, I go to spring training with Pittsburgh and I didn't know what to expect. I just kept my mouth shut and paid attention. After a couple of weeks, I realized, "Hey, I can play with these guys."

And I had to thank old Casey for that. He taught me well. I have thought a lot over the years—if he had not been my manager at the time, would I have ever made it to the major leagues?

<hr>

ART JOHNSON, *left-handed pitcher on Stengel's Boston Braves, 1940–42.*

He enjoyed teaching rookies. Didn't have too much time for the old veterans, who were probably on their way down. He thought they should know everything. He'd get very upset with them if they made mental errors.

But as far as the rookies were concerned, he had all the time in the world to teach us. He had patience with us. He was just a great manager.

He was very much fun to be around. Not only fun, but he was instructional. He was always talking baseball, always teaching you.

He taught me a lot of things. Between he and a man called Duffy Lewis, who was our traveling secretary, I learned. Duffy was the old Red Sox outfielder. Between he and Casey, I learned a lot. From Duffy Lewis, I learned how to be a gentleman—how to dress, how to talk to people, how to tip in restaurants.

From Casey, I learned a lot of the right things to do as far as baseball is concerned. The fundamentals. (He was) great for teaching fundamentals.

TOMMY HOLMES, *Boston Braves outfielder under Stengel, 1942–43:*

Number one, you couldn't get away with anything. Loafing. Fundamentals. Casey was a fundamentalist. He might like me, but if I did something wrong, I'd hear it. I liked that.

He'd get mad if somebody threw to the wrong base or whatever. If he didn't like what he saw, he'd talk to a coach. "Are you doing anything for this guy?"

Paul Waner was on our team. When I first came up, I took an 0–for–9 in a doubleheader. Oh, God! An 0–for–9! I'm screaming, you know?

Who sits besides me, having a beer? Casey. He says, "What's the matter, kid?"

I said, "An 0–for–9. I'll take one or two, but 0–for–9."

He says, "Come out in the morning."

Casey got Paul for me. "Waner," he says, "work with Tommy."

If Casey couldn't teach you something, he got you the teachers.

First baseman **MOOSE SKOWRON**, *who played on Stengel's New York Yankees, 1954–60:*

I wouldn't have been in the big leagues if it wasn't for Casey Stengel.

He told me when I first worked out with the Yankees, "Moose, you sign up with the Yankees and I'll have you here in three years."

He did. He wanted to give a younger player a chance. He believed in that.

He was a great guy. When he'd talk to you guys, the press, he'd dazzle you guys. Right? When he talked to the ballplayers, he'd talk real plain English. He gave me hell.

I remember I was leading the club in double plays. I was pulling everything. Casey called me into his office. He closed the door. He said, "Moose, you're going to learn how to hit that ball to right field with a man on first with no outs, or a man on second, or your ass is going to be back in the minor leagues."

I learned how to hit that ball to right field.

At Yankee Stadium, when I hit a ground ball and it was going to be a double play, I could see Casey's cap go from the left side of the dugout to the right side of the dugout. He was coming after me.

I hit one ball to right field, and the second baseman made a helluva play and threw to the shortstop and they made a double play. Casey came after me.

I said, "I can't *steer* the damn thing!" That was it. He turned around and walked away from me.

The guy made me what I am today.

<hr>

RON SWOBODA, of Stengel's 1965 New York Mets:

I watched him like a hawk. I was in awe of him. I never thought he was silly or irrelevant. I thought he was wise and patient.

He was just amazing to be around. He knew so much baseball, it was silly. He understood that you didn't know the game. He understood that you needed to learn the game.

He let me play. He gave me every opportunity. He said, "Hell, you ain't going to learn how to hit these pitchers sitting on the bench."

He worked with me. What he wanted me to do when I was younger was to learn more fundamental things. Like, when you throw the ball in, keep it down. Bend down when you throw. He used to say, "When you follow through after you throw the ball, bend down like you're picking grass."

I took it to heart. This is Casey Stengel talking to you during spring training.

So I'm out there working on this. Because he told me that we need to keep the ball down, I'm working on it by throwing towards the clubhouse in old Huggins-Stengel Field. There's the door to his office there. It had three glass panels in it.

I was working with Carlton Willey, the old pitcher. Somebody was hitting me balls. I was coming up with them and throwing and bending over and trying to follow through. And keeping the ball down.

Well, I didn't keep one of them down, and it went over Carlton Willey's head. It went all the way to the locker room and went right through the glass door to Stengel's office.

There was this wonderful little round hole. It was opaque glass. I could see the silhouette of Stengel when the ball went crashing through. He came over and looked out through the hole in the glass. And who is in the bull's-eye of the hole but my dumb ass.

Here's a guy who had been in baseball for fifty years at this time. And I probably look like the dumb-est, greenest rookie that he has ever seen.

PHOTO COURTESY OF BOB CASE

Casey as a twenty-two-year-old rookie outfielder with the 1912 Brooklyn Dodgers. The young student of the game would go on to become one of its foremost scholars, with a strong urge to teach green players baseball's finer points.

In 1951, Stengel got the stodgy New York brass to let him set up a prep program to tutor young, up-and-coming, green Yankees. Outfielder **SAM SUPLIZIO** *was a New York farmhand in the 1950s and attended the remedial course, known as the Instructional School:*

Casey had this whole routine. And there are a lot of ex-Yankees who do this when they're coaching, to this day.

He began lecturing with you in the dugout. In the dugout, he teaches you how to watch the opposing pitchers warm up. How to watch what they're throwing. What their stuff looks like. Which way they're pitching—into the wind or with the wind at their back.

He always advised you to watch infield (practice). The other team always took infield in those days. Watch the arms of the outfielders, the arms of the infielders, the catcher. Who looked hurt and wasn't hurt. Who could run and who couldn't run—especially in the outfield, when they go in the gap after a ball.

Study the whole defensive alignment of the opposition of the day. In case they don't have regular players and they have substitutes.

That was the dugout. The next step was up to the on-deck circle.

You're kneeling in the on-deck circle. You're the next hitter. While you're there, of course, you're studying the pitcher first. You want to know what he looks like, stuff-wise. What is he featuring today? You look at the situation in the game. You got a man on first base, nobody out. You know the hitter is trying to get him over to second. Your job is going to be to drive him in from second base.

And you anticipate, if a hitter makes an out, what your job is going to be. So you are always staying ahead of the game while you're in the on-deck circle. You're not just kneeling down on one knee, swinging bats. You are watching the play of the team playing against you. You are watching what you have to do, anticipating.

Those words are in there, while he's delivering it in his own style. You know, he'd say, "You be in the dugout watching, not in the clubhouse talking to your dolly making a date for after the game. Your job is to be in the dugout, studying."

He would add the funniest damn stories. I'll never forget. He said, "You've got to pay attention. Look what happen to me. I didn't pay attention once, and a car hit me. Damn near killed me."

He'd say, "You're not peeking through holes to look at the dollies in the seats."

So now you're up at the plate. You're hitting. Now

you've got to know what your job is. A guy has doubled, you've got to move him to third. A guy's on first, two out, you've got to swing the bat for an extra-base hit. You've got to try to hit the ball hard in the gap.

Now he says, "Let's go to first base."

Now we're at first base. He says, "For some of you slow bastards who can't run, you don't have to worry about getting off the bag too far, 'cause you ain't going anywhere anyhow." The guys who can run, they could get a bigger lead.

And this is where I first heard this: There are base stealers and base runners. A base stealer would be DiMaggio. Base runners would be like a Yogi Berra.

The difference is, the runner has got to know that after the pitch is made, he has to take a bigger lead on his secondary lead, so he can go first to third on a single. Where a DiMaggio could run like hell. They were always running.

He would go through the routine, that you've got to know as a base runner that you're not a base stealer, but by getting a good secondary jump, you could still break up a double play. But you have to get back quick, or they'll pick you off.

He'd say, "Down here, a lot of my guys are peeking and waving at the girls in the box seats and looking up their skirts. You've got to keep your head out of the stands, boys, or you'll get your head up your butt."

We'd walk to second.

The most important thing at second base is knowing the arms of the outfielders. And knowing your own hitter. You've got to know where they play that hitter.

Let's say Phil Rizzuto was hitting. You had to know where the outfielders were playing him—shallower than they would the big hitters. So if they played shallow, you've got to get a big jump off second base to score. Know your hitter and where they're playing him. DiMaggio's up, and I'm a cinch to score on a single because they're playing him deep.

Then you go to third base.

He was the best at teaching you how to score from third base on a ground ball to the infield. He taught that when you take a lead down the third-base line, take it in foul territory. Go down the line as far as you can. And when you come back, you turn in onto the field, and the catcher has only your back to throw to. So you go down in foul and come back in fair. That way you get a lot of over-throws. The catcher is throwing right through your back.

Now, Stengel taught this, and I loved it: When the pitcher throws the ball, you don't know if it's a fastball or a curveball, but you can read up and down—if it's low or high. He talked about the up-and-down of the pitch. It was the first time I ever heard it.

It's right there. When it's low, you can take an extra couple of steps to the plate, because that's going to be a ground ball. Eight out of ten times that's a ground ball on a low pitch.

If it's high, don't go as far, maybe even hold your ground, to tag up. Because high balls are what you want to drive in a run on a fly ball with less than two out.

You would never have heard any of that unless you talked to a Stengel guy. And they don't even teach it today.

I'm telling you, the Yankees drilled it. And they could score from third like nobody's business.

That was my first real listening to Casey Stengel. I used every bit of it when I was coaching in the major leagues, and they asked me to work with players on base running. I have it all written down somewhere.

Utility man **ROD KANEHL,** *a Yankees farmhand who later played under Stengel on the 1962–64 Mets:*

I was in the Yankees rookie camp in 1954. I really hadn't had much exposure to baseball, except to play American Legion ball. I didn't play in high school. I had tools, but they weren't very refined.

Casey was in charge. He ran the show. It was tremendous. It was my first exposure to professional baseball. Casey had installed a system of development of players—everyone would play a certain way. This way, when players were promoted from B ball to A ball, they were all in sync.

In the first few days of the camp, he would take you to home plate. A whole group of players. He said the whole object of the game was to start at home and get back to home as quick as possible. "That's how simple this game is."

He was very entertaining. He was a smart man. He was very practical. And he loved young players.

He would show you how to take signs, how to decoy. You look at the first-base coach and out to the outfield and just swing your head around, and at the same time the third-base coach is giving the signs. If there's a runner on base, he's doing the same thing. Everybody's catching the signs at the same time.

Then you'd go down to first, and he'd show you how to lead off first, how to check your outfield. It was just a very systematic way of playing the game. You'd go to second, and he'd do the same thing. Leading off second, how to round third. Then how to lead off third.

Some people understood and some people didn't.

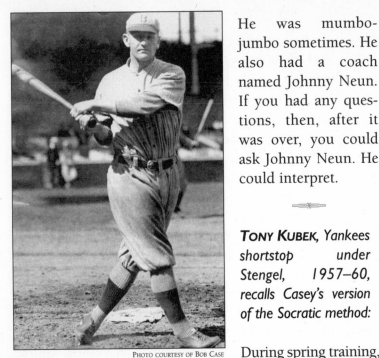

Photo courtesy of Bob Case

Casey swings a bat for Brooklyn, where he studied under legendary Dodgers manager Uncle Wilbert Robinson. Stengel also arranged to have his mentor hit in the face with a grapefruit dropped from an airplane.

He was mumbo-jumbo sometimes. He also had a coach named Johnny Neun. If you had any questions, then, after it was over, you could ask Johnny Neun. He could interpret.

TONY KUBEK, *Yankees shortstop under Stengel, 1957–60, recalls Casey's version of the Socratic method:*

During spring training, and sometimes after an off-day, we would have to report to the ballpark early for what Casey called his "Instructual School."

He would start off sitting on a stool in front of his locker. "What am I thinking about?" he would ask.

"I'm thinking: Who's starting for them tonight? What does he throw? What pitch do I want to hit? Can I bunt on their third baseman? What kind of arms do their outfielders have? What hand do they wear their gloves on? Does the pitcher have good control? Can I hit-and-run on him? Who are their relievers?"

He kept going on and on.[1]

Casey revived the Instructional School with the historically bad expansion Mets, many of whom were green as in young, others who were green as in moldy. **ROD KANEHL:**

When I was with the Mets, there were very few American Leaguers in spring training. Casey would go through the spiel again. Take everybody to first base and go around the bases, just like he did with the Yankees.

We had some old-timer National Leaguers, you know. Hodges and Craig and Labine and Ashburn. They were going through this as if they were rookies. Casey's going through the same thing, and he doesn't bat an eye. They're not snickering. They're very attentive and they're very interested. They had never heard this stuff before. They had never been under Stengel. They had never been around Stengel.

But now, instead of Johnny Neun explaining things, Stengel would say, "Kanehl, explain it."

He knew that I knew what he was talking about. I had seen it before.

"Kanehl, show them how to do this."

"Kanehl, show them how to do that."

"Kanehl, round second."

"Kanehl, round third."

I'm explaining these things to guys who have fifteen, twenty years in the major leagues. Ashburn—Richie Ashburn. I'm showing Richie Ashburn how to lead off first base.

They don't know me from Adam. I played Double-A ball the year before.

One day, they're bunting. Roger Craig is on the mound. He's supposed to be lobbing them in, so you can lay a bunt down, right?

Casey says, "Kanehl, show them how to bunt."

Well, these guys are tired of this. Who's this Kanehl kid?

So Roger Craig decked me.

<hr />

AL JACKSON, New York Mets left-handed pitcher, 1962–65:

Everybody knew him. Everybody knew what he had done and what he had been around. You knew that he had probably forgotten more than anyone else will ever know. You knew that going in, so you had to lend an ear.

He made my career so much easier. I learned so much from him. I didn't have an overabundance of talent, but I could maximize the talent that I had.

Everybody always said earlier that he didn't like young players. Well, he didn't like young players because they didn't do the small things consistently. That's probably why he always had old teams. He figured old guys could do the small things all the time. And the big things every once in a while. He taught old players, too. Did you pick it up, though? That's a different thing.

He would always go through the basics every spring, just basic fundamentals. And you go from there.

The way he taught the game, it was kind of a different way, a unique way that he did things. But I finally got the message.

Very seldom would he talk to you directly. He was a guy who would just be walking up and down the dugout, talking about the game. He did that every day. Every now and then he'd walk up and down the dugout and he'd be saying, "If I was a little left-handed pitcher,

I would do this. If I was a little left-handed pitcher, I would do that."

And I looked around and I was the only one there. I finally got the message that he was really talking to me.

And what was unique about him is that whenever there was a situation where he thought something should be done, he would speak about it before it would happen. Most people speak on it after it happens. He would always say what he would do before it would happen.

He talked about the situation—bang-bang-bang. Every other manager I've ever had would talk about it later. "He should of done this. He should of done that."

I think it was a little more impressive to talk about it before it happened. To do that, you had to truly believe in what you were saying. And he did.

He taught you how to play your own game. I got a lot out of that. No doubt about it. Thinking for yourself is what it was all about. You still had to go out and execute. You had to recognize situations, what to do in situations.

I think I went about seven years in the National League without a team sacrificing a man from second to third against me. Casey taught me how to execute that.

How did he do it? Ah—this is an example of how he made you think for yourself.

He made you think. He asked you, "What are people taught about that situation?"

Everyone is taught to bunt the ball down the third-base line. They know that's the proper way, because the first baseman, he can come down on you. The third baseman has to hold. The pitcher has to throw the ball and cover the line. There's a spot on the third-base side that's vacant. That's where they execute most of the time. This is what everybody is taught.

Casey said, "They never stop to think about whether you're a right-hander or a left-hander."

See, left-handed pitchers have a little bit of an opportunity to execute this play. Left-handers fall off toward the third-base line. You can get them if you learn to throw the ball on the run. So I went out and practiced throwing that way.

He also told me if you throw a slider and take some speed off, it will give you another two steps to get toward that line. So just throw the ball inside, because most hitters, whether they're pitchers or position players, will bunt at anything you throw. Because basically they don't want to bunt.

So now all you do is take a little off a slider to a right-hand hitter and throw it inside and make him bunt down the third-base line.

This was all from Casey. He was just talking. Just talking. And I was the only one sitting there.

TOMMY BYRNE, *left-handed pitcher on Stengel's Yankees, 1949–51, 1954–57:*

He might make a remark in the clubhouse or a remark on the bench, and he won't refer to a particular person, but that person would be somewhere in earshot. And that's how that person and the rest of the guys would pick up on it.

There are always some students who get left behind.
EDDIE JOOST, *infielder with Stengel's 1943 Braves:*

I can say honestly that there was nothing he did that helped me. He never spoke to me about things that I was not doing correctly. He wasn't like that. It was just, "You go out and play. You don't play well, to hell with you. We'll put somebody else in there."

⚊⬦⚊

In a lecture setting, Stengel could be at times entertaining, at times overwhelming. He often instructed via parables. He often delivered them via parabolas. You needed to sit up straight and pay attention. Eyes front. **RUGGER ARDIZOIA** *pitched for Stengel on the '46 Oakland Oaks:*

Casey used to tell us stories about the old days. He used to raise his finger when he was talking. I remember him talking about a guy named Germany Schaefer. Casey really like him.

Sometimes you wanted to go out there and warm up, but you had to wait until Casey finished his stories. Casey was a pretty shrewd baseball man. He tried to teach us as much as he could with those stories.

⚊⬦⚊

HY HURWITZ, *who covered Stengel's Braves for the* Boston Globe:

From 1938 up to World War II, I spent considerable time traveling with Casey and listening to him talk of his days and his pranks with the Dodgers, the Pirates, the Giants, and the Braves as a player. All you had to do is listen and you'd learn something new, something unusual, and something intriguing every day.[2]

⚊⬦⚊

Bobby Brown, *Yankees infielder under Stengel,*
1947–54:

You had to listen carefully, because a lot of times the conversation was pretty wild. Usually, if you kept close attention, there was a pearl or two in there.

You had to make sure you got it when he dropped it.

Art Johnson:

I heard a million stories. We'd sit in the lobby at night when we were on the road, and we'd just listen to Casey tell baseball stories. All of his stories had some wisdom in them. There was always a reason for telling you the story.

Casey's mentor was John McGraw. He loved John McGraw. He learned a lot of baseball from John McGraw. You could pretty much tell. He was about McGraw's size. He kind of walked like McGraw, and every once in a while, he'd refer to him. When he was telling you something, he would say, "As Mr. McGraw told me . . ."

"When I was talking to Mr. McGraw, he told me . . ."

You could tell that McGraw was in the background all the time.

Bob Sales, *who covered Stengel's Mets with the*
New York Herald Tribune:

You could follow him around. He was like the Pied Piper. The previous generation of people thought he was a clown. They didn't listen to what he was saying.

Casey was from the generation when people entertained themselves by telling stories, because it was pre-television and pre-radio and all that. He talked in metaphors. And he had this enormous collection of stories that he would tell about his old roommate, Leon Cadore, and how he was introduced to Edna, and all that.

And there was always a little bit of wisdom. Because he was not a clown. He was a smart guy.

—————

TOMMY BYRNE:

He had a background of being kind of outgoing and telling funny stories. Almost flaky stuff.

A lot of times he'd tell those things in the clubhouse or on the bench when they weren't apropos. It seemed like he was trying to get the players to relax a little bit, without telling them to relax. He'd relate to us something that happened twenty years before.

—————

*Infielder **SIBBY SISTI** played for Stengel on the Boston Braves, 1939–42:*

He was always talking with Phil Masi and myself, telling us stories. We used to get on the train to go from one city to another. He would corner Phil and myself, because we were two young guys. He'd be talking baseball all the time.

As far as I'm concerned, he gave me my break in life. He called me up from Hartford when I was only eighteen years old. He gave me my start.

He always treated me well. The other guys used to kid

me and Phil about being Casey's pets. The fact was, he had hopes that we would become pretty good ballplayers someday. He was going to teach us.

Some of the older guys, he might have got a little teed off and disgusted with them. Being a green rookie, just eighteen, he had a lot of patience with me.

RON SWOBODA:

I used to listen to him. He would regale the writers. I mean, he would *regale* them. He'd tell them stories. And if you listened to his stories, the guys he was talking about had played forty, fifty years before. And the stories were parables. They were things that he was trying to tell you about.

But he saw you listening. And he's telling the writers these stories. The idea was, he saw you listening.

Instead of haranguing you about something over and over again, somehow the story meanders into something that he wants you to listen to.

It was a parable.

JACK LANG, who covered Stengel's Yankees and Mets for the Long Island Press:

Casey told us this: He played for the Brooklyn Dodgers, and the manager in those days was a guy named Wilbert Robinson. He was a short, fat guy. A baggy uniform.

He was furious that his players couldn't bunt. He would send them up to bunt and they would foul one off.

One of them one day says to Robinson, "If it's so easy, why don't you go up and do it?"

So in batting practice, Wilbert Robinson goes up, this old man—he's in his sixties at the time—he goes up and the pitcher throws, and he lays down a perfect bunt.

As he's walking back to the dugout, Wilbert Robinson says, "See? It's as easy as jacking off. Once you learn how, you never forget."

Casey used to tell us that story.

AL JACKSON:

That was another way of getting people's attention. His stories. He could do that so well.

I remember in San Francisco one night, a fog came in during the third inning. It stopped the game. This was in our first year, and you've got a whole lot of strange people on the team. Nobody really knew one another real well. We just hadn't been together that long.

So we walk back into the clubhouse, and everybody is kind of in their lockers. You might have been talking to your locker neighbor, or something like that.

And Casey just took a chair and set it in the middle of the room. And he just started talking. Not to any individual. No one was around him when he started talking.

Everybody started to look around, and there's that old man sitting in the middle of the room in a chair, talking. It wasn't a matter of a minute or two before all twenty-five players were sitting around him on the floor, just like little kids. He was amazing. He was just talking and talking. I think he told us ten stories. Ten stories!

The stories were good, too. But he would start the first story, get halfway, and start another one.

He did that all the way through. There might have been three stories that you were really interested in. But you had to wait until he came back to finish them.

SAM SUPLIZIO:

I used to watch him at the winter meetings at the Fountainbleau Hotel in Miami. A lot of us would go down there and see what was going on.

No matter what time of day you went into the Fountainbleau, he was there. It could be two in the afternoon. It could be midnight. It could be two o'clock in the morning. Casey held court.

Everybody would say, "Who is in the middle of that crowd over there?"

It was Casey Stengel. Telling stories.

ROD DEDEAUX:

I always understood everything he said. And I've often said that it always bothered me that I was the only one who always understood.

If you knew what to listen for, you could always understand him. He'd be talking sense, but on more than one subject.

Out here, probably our number-one sportswriter, he was a feature writer as well, was Braven Dyer. He was the dean of the sportswriters. He was with the *L.A. Times*. They had sort of a party. Casey was managing the Yankees at the time, and a local person coming back from the Yankees was big news.

On this occasion, we were sitting down at this round table and Casey was holding court. Braven was at the table. We had been sitting there for over an hour.

Braven was next to me and he says, "Now I want to show you something. I'm supposed to be the top sportswriter. I listen to people and write great stories. I've been sitting here listening to Casey for over an hour, and I'm enthralled at what he's saying. But do you want to see the notes that I've written?"

He showed me. His pad was blank. There wasn't anything that he could really write down. He got it. He grasped what he said. But writing it down, trying to duplicate it, was an impossibility.

That to me typifies Casey's storytelling better than anything.

***

TIM HORGAN, *then a reporter for the* **Boston Herald-Traveler***, sat in on some of Stengel's dugout seminars in the 1950s:*

There was one thing about Casey that I found out from Arthur Siegel, my editor at the *Traveler*. You go up to him in the dugout before a game and you ask him a question, Arthur said, "But don't expect an answer. Don't move. Sooner or later, he'll answer your question. It might take five minutes; it might be when you're going back to the clubhouse. But he'll answer it. You just have to sweat him out."

The first question I ever asked him, in the Fenway dugout, was why Mickey Mantle didn't bat right-handed at the Fens all the time, to take advantage of the wall. Stengel responded with a discourse on the quality of the infield sod at Kankakee, Illinois, in 1910 and kept it up until game time.

After the game, I just chanced to visit his office in the clubhouse. He looked up when I walked in and said, "I'll tell you why. Because Mantle ain't used to batting right-handed against a righty pitcher, so why should I mess him up just for one park?"

Casey paused and then added gently, "But I got to say I thunk about that, too."

⊷⊶

Stengel knew how to conjure real-life applications for the course material. **ROD KANEHL:**

Casey was a very practical guy. I go to spring training the second year, I'm standing around with the pitchers. He's talking to one of them. He's asking him, "What was your record last year?"

Casey knows his record. It was a rhetorical question. Before he could answer, Casey says, "Well, you don't have a changeup. If you'd had a changeup, you would have won three more of those games that you lost. And instead of making seventeen thousand dollars, you'd be making twenty-three thousand." He put things in dollars and cents.

He said to me, "You run good. You should get ten more hits a year bunting. Instead of hitting .245, you'd be hitting .265. And instead of making your eleven thousand dollars, you'd be making fifteen thousand." Very practical. He talked to players that way.

One time at the Polo Grounds, some guy was trying to sell a record at supermarkets. He was going to have the Mets do something or another. We were going to either get a thousand dollars each now or a percentage later.

After the fellow left, we were all talking about what we should do. Take the money or take the percentage?

Casey said, "I just want to say one thing. That a hundred percent of nothing is nothing. Take the thousand dollars now." He had probably seen so many of those deals.

ART JOHNSON:

You know what he used to do every year? There was a man who owned a Plymouth dealership on Commonwealth Avenue. We always seemed to have five or six players from California, and we always seemed to have a few who lived on the West Coast.

I saw Casey buy as many as eight brand-new Plymouths at one time. These fellows would drive them back to California. And then when Casey would get them back in California, he would sell them at an excellent profit.

I learned a lot from Casey as far as learning how to handle your own finances. He was a smart guy as far as finances were concerned. He'd give you a lot of hints. He'd talk to you about saving your money.

Some lessons didn't sink in for years. WHITEY HERZOG, the baseball brain and successful manager with the Texas Rangers, Kansas City Royals, and Saint Louis Cardinals, was a Yankees minor leaguer in the 1950s:

One time in spring training, we had the hit-and-run on, and Carl Erskine threw me a curve and I struck out into a double play.

I came back to the bench and Casey said, "Next time, tra-la-la."

I didn't know what tra-la-la meant, but next time up I hit a line drive, right into a double play. When I sat down, Casey came over and said, "Like I told you. Tra-la-la."[3]

***

SAM SUPLIZIO:

He'd say, "You want to win? You gotta make your guys feel good. They feel good, they laugh. They tra-la-la."

You know, he saw you when you were tight, trying too hard. I can remember a couple of guys hitting, in just exhibition games.

He'd say, "Time out a minute.

"Hey, doctor. Just tra-la-la."

Until you're older, you don't really know what he's talking about. But if you think about it, he really meant, "Hey—have fun. Take it easy. Don't be pressured. Tra-la-la. Just relax."

Now you realize he knew what he was saying.

***

Casey liked to keep his students sharp, on their toes.
He pulled pop quizzes. **ART JOHNSON:**

When he'd come out to the mound, first thing he'd say was, "How're you feeling, kid?"

Kid. He always had problems with names.

"Well, I'm doing fine."

"You think you can hang in there another couple of innings?" In those days, we did not have any middle

relievers, short or long relievers, closers. You were a
starter and a reliever. You'd start today, rest tomorrow, and
the next day you'd be in the bullpen until it was time for
you to start again.

Casey was always interested in how you were feeling.
Physically and mentally.

He'd ask you some questions. Who's coming up? How
many men on base now? Do you remember?

You'd say, "Yeah, I've got two men on."

"How many outs?"

He wanted to make sure that you focused right in on
the game and knew exactly what the status was and what
position you were in.

TOMMY BYRNE:

He'd come up to the young fellows and scare them to
death. He'd just walk up to two or three of them who were
standing by themselves, and he'd already start putting the
screws to them. Talking to them in ways that would try to
make them more alive, more alert.

RON HUNT, *infielder on Stengel's Mets, 1963–65:*

He'd come up and say something funny. Give you a little
zinger and move on.

RALPH HOUK, *a backup catcher and later coach on
Stengel's Yankees:*

When I first came back with the Yankees as a coach, we were still traveling by train. The coaches would always sit with him for dinner on the train. Casey liked to sit in there and have a few cocktails after he ate.

Since I was the newest coach, they said, "It's your job now to sit in there with him. We can't let him sit in there by himself."

It so happened that one day he said to me, "Ralph, what do you think about the hit-and-run?"

I said, "Well, in some cases, I think it's a pretty good play."

He said, "It's a terrible play." And he proceeded to spend about ten minutes telling me why it was no good.

It was about a week or so later and we were on the train again. And he said, "Ralph, what do you think of the hit-and-run?"

I said, "Well, I'm not too fond of it. I don't like it too well."

He said, "Ralph, it's the greatest play that there is in baseball."

Then he spent about ten minutes telling me what a great play it was.

***

Think outside the box, question established practices, experiment with new ideas. Stengel could be a radical scholar.

His most controversial philosophy was platooning—juggling players in and out of the lineup, from day to day or inning to inning, depending upon game situations, matchups, or just plain hunches. Stengel picked up the notion from his mentor, John McGraw—who had platooned Casey.

MEL DUEZABOU *played outfield for Stengel's*
Oakland Oaks:

I was a right-handed hitter. It was the first time I ever
heard of a right-handed batter not being able to hit a
right-handed pitcher.

If a left-handed pitcher was pitching, I was in the
lineup. If a right-handed pitcher was pitching, I was not
in the lineup.

His theory is just what they all do now. He platooned.
It was the first time I had ever heard of it.

Stengel mastered the theory three years into his
tenure with the Yankees, when he felt more com-
fortable using platooning and other unconventional
methods on the very conventional ball club.

For instance, in Game 6 of the 1951 World
Series, the Yankees protected a 4–1 lead in the
ninth. With the bases loaded and none out, and
righty sluggers Monte Irvin and Bobby Thomson due
up, the Baseball Textbook says bring in a right-
handed reliever.

Stengel brought in lefty Bob Kuzava, who retired
Irvin, Thomson, and righty pinch-hitter Sal Yvars.
BOBBY BROWN:

We all got along with him well, but he had the platoon
system. So nobody who wasn't playing every day was ever
happy. That was normal.

I don't think anyone doubted that this guy knew what
the heck he was doing. He did screwy things, but they had
good reasoning when you sat down and thought about it.

He would have different ideas. I remember when he brought in Kuzava against the Giants. He got out of the jam and we won the Series. He wouldn't hesitate to do stuff like that.

He toyed with the idea of putting all left-handed hitters against (Dusty) Parnell up in Fenway Park, because Parnell broke the bats of the right-handers. Stuff like that. He was always thinking.

I always thought he managed left-handed but managed well. He just did things that were different.

TOMMY HOLMES:

I was at Yankee Stadium when they were in the World Series against the Dodgers. This would have been '53, I guess.

The Dodgers had all them right-handed hitters, Jackie Robinson. Casey leaves Kuzava in. I'm second-guessing him. I'm thinking, *Oh, boy! Leaving in the left-hander.* And with that bullpen he had.

Kuzava won. He saved the game.

ART JOHNSON:

He didn't worry about left-handers pitching against right-handers or right-handers pitching against left-handers. He didn't worry about things like that. His feeling was, if you were a decent pitcher, you could pitch against left-handers and right-handers.

I pitched against Ted Williams and Stan Musial, hitters like that. They didn't care if it was a left-hander or a right-hander pitching. Casey didn't care about it either.

A lot of people say anybody could win with the talent he had with the Yankees. Well, I don't think that's true.

Casey did a lot of things. He was instrumental in the platoon system. He started it.

Sure, he had some great players in New York. But he made them winners.

———

Tinker, try new things, explore. Stengel knew that true scholarship is a lifetime pursuit. **RALPH HOUK:**

We were in spring training. In early spring training, you'd have different workouts and different things that you want to work on.

We were working on a play where you get a runner caught between home and third base. I don't know where he came up with the idea, but he came up with some kind of an idea where you'd throw it to a different person every time. You'd have the shortstop come and replace the third baseman, and the catcher would go here, and the pitcher would cover home. He had everybody so confused by the time we got done working at it, we just didn't know what to do. We even had the second baseman get into the play. And the first baseman backing up the play.

The next day he said, "You know, I don't think we ought to work on that play anymore." He wouldn't say it was a bad play. He just said he thought we'd worked on that play enough. That was the last we ever heard of it.

He was always coming up with something.

———

BOBBY RICHARDSON, *second baseman on Stengel's Yankees, 1955–60:*

He'd pinch-hit for a guy who was 3–for–3. He would take out a right-handed hitter against a left-handed pitcher (and) put in a left-handed pinch-hitter. But he had so much talent, it would usually work out for him.

***

HANK BAUER, *outfielder for Stengel's Yankees, 1949–59:*

Once he pinch-hit for me with the bases loaded and nobody out in the first inning!

And one day we were playing in Detroit. Jackie Jensen was with the team then. Jackie hit a home run and a double. I hit two home runs and a double. And the score was tied, 5–5, in the top of the eighth or the top of the ninth.

He sent Gene Woodling up to pinch-hit for me. I almost knocked Gene's legs off with the bat.

I got in the dugout, and Casey came up to me and he says, "I thought you'd reached your quota."

***

He knew his students and their capabilities. Stengel could be demanding. He expected a lot from the best. **RAY BERRES,** *catcher for Stengel's 1935 Brooklyn Dodgers:*

At times he could be entertaining, and at times he could be a little feisty, too. When I say feisty, I mean he could be strict and stern.

> ⊰⊱

JERRY COLEMAN, *infielder on Stengel's Yankees, 1949–57:*

I was with him on the Far East tour in '55. He was running back and forth in the dugout like a lunatic. He was driving everybody crazy.

After a while, the bench was empty. The entire non-playing team went down to sit in the bullpen to get away from him. He was just as interested in winning those games as he was in the World Series.

> ⊰⊱

GEORGE SULLIVAN, *who served as visiting-team bat-boy at Fenway Park in the fabled summer of 1949:*

This was his first season as manager of the Yankees. He had a real challenge that first year to prove to people that George Weiss, who had hired him, was right and the critics were wrong.

That season was such a famous one, the summer of '49. Luckily enough, I had a front-row seat to the whole thing when the two principal teams got together in Boston.

The Yankees had a pretty big lead in midseason, and the Red Sox started to come like gangbusters from July on. They were almost unbeatable at Fenway. So here we come, August into September, and the Red Sox are chipping away, chipping away.

Finally, we come to the last game of the Red Sox home season. A Sunday. The Red Sox had won the first two games of the series. We're down to the last Sunday of the home season.

If the Red Sox win this, it's a dead heat. A tie between the two teams.

It was a real big ball game.

In the top of the second inning, Tommy Henrich hooked a line drive over Billy Goodman's head into the right-field corner. He got a double out of it. Billy Johnson grounded out to (Bobby) Doerr, with Henrich moving over to third base.

Johnny Lindell, the outfielder, was up next. A power hitter to all fields. Lindell hit a tremendous high fly to deep right field, just near the warning track. Al Zarilla went back to the bullpen.

He threw to the plate.

I went up from the on-deck circle to pull the bat out of the way. There's going to be a play at the plate.

Birdie Tebbetts, who's catching, is giving it the wooden-Indian trick. Staring into space, hands at your side, as if the ball's not coming.

It was a fantastic throw, all the way from deep right field. Head high.

Here comes Tommy Henrich pounding down the line. And at the last split-second, Birdie flashes into action, takes the ball right in front of his forehead, and twists. Tommy sees at the last minute what's going on, and he starts a belated slide.

He was out. Tommy gave a half-hearted complaint to the umpire, because I suspect he knew he was out.

It was a crucial play in the ball game. That cut off the Yankees run and kept it scoreless. The Red Sox went on to win, 4–1.

On a play like that, of course, the home-base coach is the on-deck hitter, and that was Charlie Silvera. What they're supposed to do is get down on their hands and knees if the base runner is supposed to slide.

The crowd noise is tremendous. If you yell, "Get down, get down," chances are the guy won't hear you. Charlie Silvera did not get down on his hands and knees.

We go back to the dugout. The inning is over.

Casey just unloaded on Silvera, giving him what-for. I mean, he really unloaded on him.

Charlie was saying, "I was yelling. I was yelling." And Casey, in reading the riot act to him, told him he had to get down on that play.

I remember being shocked by it, the way he talked to Silvera. It just wasn't the Casey I had known.

***

TOMMY BYRNE:

Although he cut up and carried on a little bit, he was serious as hell about trying to get the players we had to pull together, to play together.

When we might be down three runs, and folks might be tired, it might be hot. He'd get off of that goddamn bench and he'd be yelling like a kid. He'd start swinging that left arm around and everything.

"Let's go get 'em," and that sort of thing.

Some of the guys realized that maybe he has got something. Let's see if we can't go get it for him.

He wasn't one to sit around and die on the vine if we got behind.

He was always throwing those left hooks around the dugout. Whatever the circumstances: "Let's get one. Let's hit one out of here. Let's get this goddamn game going." He was trying to get everybody jacked up again.

For folks that didn't know him, they probably thought

he didn't have it all together. The middle-of-the-road guys, it would relax them. But the old guys, they didn't like being behind, and it was almost like he was casting aspersions on them.

But he'd have some comment that would get people woke up. He was trying to give them the red-ass.

MARK FREEMAN, *a pitcher in the Yankees system in the late 1950s:*

He called me into his office when I made the Yankees in '59. Casey didn't like the way I held people on first base. Or, as he put it, *didn't* hold people on first base.

He had a beanbag paperweight that was real heavy on his desk. And he called me in there and he said, "Watch this."

He wanted me to leap up in the air and turn as I throw it. To show me how to do it, he threw that beanbag at me as hard as he could throw it. It hit me in the chest.

Casey said, "Now let me have it again. I want you to watch how I do this."

I knew what he was doing. He was just throwing it at me because he was mad at me for the way I was holding on runners.

HANK BAUER:

I remember one day we played a doubleheader. This was probably in '49 or '50 in old Shibe Park, Philadelphia. And we got beat both games.

We jumped on a train after the game and we were in

the dining car. Rizzuto started this: We started playing Twenty Questions.

And Casey came in and, oh goddamn, did he blow his top. He said, "If you had shown this much enthusiasm at the ballpark, we wouldn't have dropped the double-header."

You could hear a pin drop. We all ate our meal and got the hell out of that dining room in a hurry.

Besides his stop with Stengel's '43 Braves, **EDDIE JOOST** *was a distinguished shortstop for several other major-league teams, mostly the Cincinnati Reds and Philadelphia Athletics, 1936–55. Joost:*

I was playing with Philadelphia. He used to hate to see us. If you go back and look, we used to beat the Yankees. In '48, '49, and even '50.

One day I hit a home run in the ninth inning to tie the game. I looked over, and Stengel jumped up and hit his head on the dugout roof. He nearly knocked himself out. He was just screaming.

Another time, I get to second base and Rizzuto is standing there. I said, "Hey, Phil. How's things?"

He said, "Don't talk to me."

I said, "What the hell is the matter?"

He said, "DON'T TALK TO ME. He'll fine me."

I said, "What do you mean, he'll fine you?"

"Never mind."

And he walked away.

I used to kid with Yogi all the time. So the next time I go up to bat, I tapped his shinguards with my bat and said, "Hey, Yog. What's going on?"

He said, "Don't talk to me."

Finally, I get out to second base again, and I said to Phil, "What the hell is going on?"

He said, "Stengel says if he catches any of us talking to you guys, he'll fine us. Stengel said, 'These guys go out there and give you the buddy-buddy treatment. And all they do is go out there and beat your ass every day.'"

I hear it was because after they lost a doubleheader to us, and they were on the train from Philadelphia to Washington, they were laughing and having a few beers and having a good time. And Stengel just gave them hell. He just gave them hell. "All you do is talk to these guys, and all they do is beat the hell out of you."

~~~

JERRY COLEMAN:

I used to listen to him when he'd come out and argue with the umpires. "You're stealing from my men! You're stealing from my men! You're a thief!" He was very serious about winning.

~~~

RUGGER ARDIZOIA, who pitched for Stengel with the Oakland Oaks:

When he'd come out to argue with the umpire, he'd get right up in their face. The umpires wore those old masks. Casey had a pretty big nose. He'd get right up there and stick his nose in that mask. He gave it to them pretty good.

~~~

In Brooklyn (record under Casey: 208–251), Boston (373–491), and with the Mets (175–404), he was definitely stuck with the baseball version of the dumb class. **TOMMY HOLMES:**

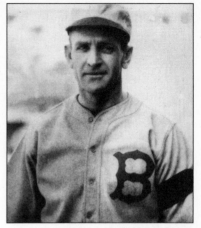

PHOTO FROM THE AUTHOR'S COLLECTION

Casey as manager of the Brooklyn Dodgers. The team was strong on wackiness, short on talent, and Stengel began to gain a reputation as a clownish manager.

I remember Philadelphia came in on Opening Day one year.

Casey says to us, "I know who's going to finish last." He meant the Phillies.

And somebody says, "Yeah. And we'll be second last."

In other words, on Opening Day, we had our place already picked out. Because we didn't have the talent.

***

SIBBY SISTI:

I played for Casey for four years, and we finished seventh each year. We were happy that the Phillies were in the league, because they finished eighth.

***

So Stengel graded on a curve. **ART JOHNSON:**

He knew exactly what talent he had. He used it as best he could. But when we lost, he wasn't that disappointed.

The owners of the team, they didn't expect Casey to finish in the top four. It would have been a miracle if they had.

He did the best with what he had. It wasn't easy, losing more than we were winning. Everyone tried to keep their cool. I never saw Casey lose his cool about losing, never saw him get upset. He might get upset with a veteran if a veteran made a mental error, but he knew we didn't have the talent.

CLIF KEANE, *baseball writer for the* Boston Globe:

When he was with the Braves, he was always yelling at ballplayers. They'd make a mistake and he'd scream at them. He wouldn't stand for any lousy play; he'd give the guy hell for it. But they just didn't have the talent. No players.

GALEN CISCO, *who pitched for Stengel on the 1962–65 Mets:*

He was a no-nonsense guy when the game started. He wanted to win as badly as anyone else. But I think he realized what kind of a team he had, and he tried to make it as easy on the players as he could.

It bothered him to lose, but I think he realized what kind of team he had. He kind of gave way to the kind of team he had. He knew that it was impossible to be even a .500 club. If we would win one out of three against the Giants or Dodgers, it was almost like winning the pennant.

ROD KANEHL:

I hear he could be a real horse's ass with the Yankees. But with us, he was loose. With the Mets, he was loose. He realized there wasn't any reason to be tough on players; there weren't really any prospects.

We were playing 162 games and trying to be respectable.

AL JACKSON:

He knew he had a terrible ball club. I don't think he would have been that jolly if he had been with the Yankees and losing.

Stengel was one of those teachers with eyes in the back of his head. He always knew who was writing notes, who threw the chalk, who was dipping pigtails in inkwells. **Moose Skowron:**

He used to give a ball to the elevator operator. Remember when they would have the guys in the elevator? "What floor do you want?"

Casey would give the ball to the elevator operator and tell him to have anyone who came in after midnight autograph it.

When we would get in, the elevator operator would ask us to sign the ball. The next day, Casey would have the ball and he knew who the hell was out after midnight.

ROD KANEHL:

But he would warn you. George Weiss would have detectives following certain guys. Casey wouldn't say out loud that somebody might be following you. I know he called in Felix Mantilla one time and told him to watch himself, that he was being tailed.

Felix's comment was, "They better have more than one, because I'm going to wear one of them out."

ART JOHNSON:

He was a disciplinarian as far as the rules were concerned. You had to be in your room by eleven o'clock at night. Of course, we played all day games then. And he had bed checks. Duffy would go around on the road.

We'd be sitting in the lobby at five minutes of eleven, and he'd say, "Okay, that's it. We're all going to bed now."

He wouldn't necessarily go to bed the same time we did. He'd sit with George Kelly and Duffy, and they'd chat until one or two or three o'clock in the morning.

ROD KANEHL:

One time we played in Houston, and we had an off-day on Monday. We flew into Chicago, and we had spent the Sunday night in Houston.

He would always walk up and down the aisle on the plane before it would taxi for takeoff. We could never figure out why he would do that.

Until we were in Chicago. He tells the clubhouse man to tell me to come into his office. Casey started dressing me down about partying in Houston and staying out late, this and that and every other thing. He said it wasn't just in Houston, it's been in other places.

Then when he finishes, he says, "And that goes for your roommate, too." My roommate was Ron Hunt.

So the message wasn't for me. The message was for me to relay to Hunt. He was just using me as a conduit to get to Hunt. He didn't want to go directly to Hunt. Hunt could be pretty temperamental; he might react badly if Casey got on him. So Casey dressed me down and made sure I told Hunt.

But I also realized then why he walked up and down the aisles. He was looking for guys who had already pulled out pillows and started napping.

Think about it. You get on a plane and you're tired; you've had a bad night the night before, you were out late, or whatever. What's the first thing you do? You pull a pillow out before the plane taxis.

He was pretty quick. He was shrewd. He knew all the tricks.

Not all the tricks. ART JOHNSON:

I can't verify this with names or anything, but I know it happened. We left Boston, on our way to Saint Louis. For some reason or another, one of the players—and I'll leave him nameless—snuck a girl on the train. Of course, we were on these Pullman cars, with the bunk beds and so forth. And Casey used to come through and check the Pullman cars.

I remember Casey coming in the Pullman car. I remember these guys hiding this girl. And Casey never found her. Casey would pull the curtains apart to make sure that you were in bed and so forth. They hid her, and she went all the way to Saint Louis with us. He never found out about it.

Nobody ever told him.

2

STUDENTS, GOOD AND BAD

Give the fellas the credit. I couldn't have done it with football players.

— Casey Stengel

Some players thought he was exacting, difficult, maddening, cruel, demanding. A tormentor and professor who drove his players crazy.

Think of Professor Kingsfield of *The Paper Chase*.

Some thought he was wise, caring, patient, a parent-figure and teacher who knew what was best for his players. "Casey Stengel was like a father to me," said Ron Hunt.

Think of Miss Crabtree of *The Little Rascals*.

Stengel and his wife, Edna, had no children. So also think of Chipping, the childless schoolteacher from *Goodbye, Mr. Chips*, who says on his deathbed:

"I thought I heard you say 'twas a pity I never had children. But you're wrong. I have thousands of them . . . and all boys!"

You can practically hear Stengel growl, "No kids? You're full of it, and I'll tell you why. I have thousands of them . . . all ballplayers!"

Casey Stengel was like any teacher, manager, boss, drill sergeant, parent. He had favorites. And he had not-so-favorites.

And the ballplayers who served under him were like any pupils, players, recruits, workers, or sons. Some worshipped him. Some loathed him. Some hung on his every word. Some tuned him out.

They all knew what he wanted. Stengel loved and respected his field of study, and he insisted that others respect it, too. Casey's formula was simple. He wanted baseball to be played properly, with care and smarts and energy. Do that and get a gold star.

"All I want you to do," Stengel once told Billy Martin, "is bust your heinie out there."

<hr />

BOB CASE, *Casey's friend and business manager during Stengel's retirement:*

People would always ask him who was his greatest player, and he would hate to answer that question.

But he used to tell me—Berra.

He told me when the game was 2–0, Berra would hit a triple to the opposite field to knock in two runs. When the game was 12–2, Mantle would hit three home runs.

In other words, Casey thought Berra was a clutch hitter, a leader. A smart player. He used to say, "They say he reads comic books; he plays like a goddamn genius for me."

Casey loved him as a player. He said, "That guy might not be a Phi Beta Kappa, but he never made a mistake on a baseball field."

His players always knew exactly what they needed to do to get a wink, a nod, a pat on the back, a good grade: Imitate Casey. **RON HUNT** *remembers the day he barreled hard into Milwaukee Braves catcher Ed Bailey. Punches were thrown and the traditional bench-clearing baseball scrum erupted in the infield:*

Ed Bailey? I ran over him at home plate. He was a macho old fucker and I was a young kid. He was going to show that he was tough.

I remember looking over at a pile of players fighting and seeing Casey on his back, kicking. Denis Menke—once he found out it was Casey—kind of protected him a little.

But you know, Casey was out there. He wasn't sitting with his ass on the bench or with his head in the goddamn water cooler.

Casey was a baseball person. He wanted a hundred percent. He gave a hundred percent.

BOB SALES, *who covered the Mets for the* New York Herald Tribune:

He loved Rod Kanehl. He was a guy who had a certain amount of baseball sense, and he would do anything for you. He played his ass off.

Then they had Ron Hunt. He kept getting hit by pitches, and Casey liked that. Dirty uniform all the time. He liked that kind of player.

———◆———

Rod Kanehl *endeared himself to Stengel as a Yankees farmhand. All it took was a simple act of enthusiasm— he vaulted a fence one day to fetch a baseball:*

It was the spring of '54. It was during batting practice.

There was about a five-foot high barbed-wire fence in the outfield. This was at Al Lang Field; that's where the rookie camp was. Kids were out there. Balls would go over the fence and kids would reach for them.

Well, I hopped the fence to get a ball. I was a high jumper in high school. It wasn't anything to hop a five-foot fence. I retrieved the ball before the kids could get to it.

I didn't even realize that I had done anything special until the next winter. The next winter, at a hot-stove dinner back in Springfield, Tom Greenwade, the scout, told the story that I had really impressed Casey by going to retrieve that ball. That I beat the kids to it and hopped back over the fence.

Casey and I got along very well. We talked the same language. I played hard, and that's all he expected from you.

———◆———

Ron Hunt, *on how he impressed the teacher:*

It was down in spring training. I had just twisted my ankle; I was on the bench. This was before we broke camp in '63. I had a pretty bad ankle. I was working it out, working it out. And the sonuvabitch was just throbbing like hell.

I was sitting on the bench and had it propped up. Casey come down the bench and he said, "Can you play?"

I said, "Yeah!"

And he poked my foot. It hurt like a sonuvabitch.

He said, "Yeah, right."

So he goes along on his way.

Three or four innings go by and he comes over and says, "Can you hit?"

I said, "Yeah!"

He said, "Okay, I'll tell you what. The pitcher leads off the next inning. I want you to pinch-hit. You go up there, you get on base, I'll get you a pinch-runner."

I said, "Okay."

So I went up. And by God, I dribbled one up the middle for a base hit.

I got down to first base. He called time, got me a pinch-runner.

I got back to the bench. My leg was just throbbing like a sonuvabitch.

I sit down and prop my leg up. And here he comes, walking down the bench. I looked up at him. He looked down at me and he winked. And kept walking.

And that was it.

Whether that prompted me breaking camp with the club on the major-league roster as a bullpen catcher or not, I don't know.

But I'd venture to say it didn't hurt.

On May 31, 1964, the Mets and San Francisco Giants played the longest game in time (twenty-three innings in seven hours, twenty-three minutes). Stengel needed someone to step up and pitch. **GALEN CISCO:**

I remember it like it was yesterday. I had started a couple of days before. He came up to me in the twelfth inning, after using what was close to his last pitcher. It was the second game of a doubleheader.

He asked me if I could pitch a couple of innings. I said I hadn't thought of it, but I could try. I didn't even have my spikes on.

He said, "Go into the clubhouse, get your spikes on, go out to the bullpen, throw a little bit, and let me know."

I did that and I called back to the dugout and said, "Hey, I feel good. I can pitch."

So I came in during the fourteenth inning. About every two innings, he would check with me. He asked me how I felt and he said, "Now listen, I don't want to hurt you. Don't try to do more than you can. But you're my last guy. Just do the best you can."

I pitched nine innings. And after the game, he said I did a helluva job. I think that was one reason why he kind of liked me. I felt like he always thought something of me for doing that.

⊰⊱

RON HUNT, *on making a further impression:*

It was at the old ballpark in Philadelphia. There was a long runway between the ballfield and the clubhouse. It was after infield, and I was coming one way and Casey was coming the other. I think the kid who was playing second base at the time was Larry Burright. He wasn't doing very good, offensively or defensively.

I asked Casey, "Can I talk to you?"

He said, "Yeah."

I said, "Ron Hunt, Number 33."

You ask me why I said that. I remember Casey saying at a meeting that he didn't remember a lot of names, just the numbers. When a sportswriter asked him why, Casey said, "Because the numbers are always here. The names change."

I said, "Casey, I remember what you said in spring training about being dissatisfied if you weren't playing. I don't think the person out there is doing the job, and I'd like to have a chance."

He said, "Yeah? You want to play that bad, huh, kid?"

I said, "Yes sir."

He said, "Okay, you'll play tomorrow."

That's how I got my chance to play.

Stengel's platoon system won ball games and pennants, but not the hearts of the Yankees who were platooned. It was the baseball equivalent of telling kids they have to share their toys at recess. **JERRY COLEMAN:**

He played his players to the best advantage better than any manager that I have ever seen.

A lot of guys hated that. They wanted to kill him. If they caught him walking down the street, Bauer and Woodling would have taken him apart piece by piece. And a few others who were platooned.

Nobody liked it.

HANK BAUER:

He'd platoon Gene Woodling and I. I didn't like him when he did it.

Whenever I didn't play, I would get as far away from him as I possibly could. I never did say nothing to the gentleman. I just thought to myself, *He's wrong.* Because I had to hit right-handers down in the minor leagues.

He knew I didn't like it.

<hr/>

MOOSE SKOWRON:

He would disgruntle Hank and Woodling with his platoons. But that was what Casey believed in.

<hr/>

Stengel believed he was keeping certain players out of situations unsuited to their abilities. He was doing it for their own good. **LEONARD KOPPETT,** *writing in* The New York Times:

Since few players—or other human beings—have a firm objective grasp of their own shortcomings, most players didn't like it when Stengel did this. Nevertheless, in countless instances, his judgment of their abilities was proved correct, and as years went by, many former players came to admit this.[2]

<hr/>

Another Stengel favorite: a guy who could play many positions. He thought versatility was good for the player and good for the team. **MAX WEST,** *who played on Stengel's Boston Braves, 1939–42:*

In my particular case, he wanted me to do so good, he hurt me. He thought I could play all positions.

In high school, you can.

He had seen me play all different positions. In spring training, that first year I went up there, I played third base while we were barnstorming. I played right field. The next day, I may play first base. In the big leagues, it's pretty tough to do that.

Especially going from right field to first base. He did that to me in Saint Louis one time. I played right field one day and first base the next. Against the Cardinals in Saint Louis, the bases are loaded and Casey played the infield in. With Johnny Mize hitting!

PHOTO COURTESY OF JOSEPH CARLISTO

Casey raises a fist to root on his Braves. Boston's National League team was cash poor and not even close to contending. By the time he was fired after the 1943 season, Stengel was considered a manager who just could not win.

I went and gave him the glove and said *you* play first base.

It was difficult for me. It was destroying me. I couldn't do it. I couldn't sleep.

But I turned out all right. And he helped me a great deal.

Sometimes he was funny. Sometimes he would make you madder than hell.

⊰⊱

CLIF KEANE, *longtime baseball writer for the* Boston Globe:

I remember one day he took his right fielder, Hank Bauer, out of the lineup. He put Enos Slaughter in to pinch-hit for him.

Bauer took a bat and flung it into the dugout.

Enos Slaughter got a base hit to win the game.

Stengel took over the Yankees in 1949, and he inherited Joe DiMaggio the way a man picks up a stepson. DiMaggio, a darling for taciturn manager Joe McCarthy, was a proven winner, the regal presence in center field, the poster boy for solemn Yankee competence, and an international star. But injuries and age were whittling his talent. Stengel had to do some dirty work. On the surface, the situation appeared to be something like Daffy Duck bossing around Clark Gable. **JERRY COLEMAN:**

There was the word around that he and DiMaggio hated one another. They didn't hate each other. Joe had McCarthy for a long time, and suddenly you have a guy who's totally different. Joe just didn't react well to him.

The only time I saw any real problem was when Joe came to the ballpark one day and found out he was hitting fifth behind Johnny Mize. Joe didn't like that because Casey didn't talk to him about it. Apparently he didn't.

There was a cold silence between them from there on in. I don't think there was ever any warmth between them. Joe was not a warm guy anyway. Very quiet. Very into himself.

With Casey and Joe, they were two very strong personalities. Here's Joe, the super-duper star of all time, at that time. And here's Stengel coming on, with this rather unusual reputation. Kind of kooky. Of course, Casey wasn't kooky—he was brilliant.

CLIF KEANE:

DiMaggio didn't like him. At the end of his career, DiMaggio played a game at first base. Stengel was the guy who thought he should try it because he couldn't play the outfield anymore.

I remember DiMaggio worked out here at Fenway Park and Ted Williams was watching. Williams yelled out, "You won't be eating corn tonight, Joe!"

Meaning he was going to get a ground ball in the mouth. DiMaggio just glared at Ted.

Stengel was a tough guy. He made tough decisions. He was a hard-boiled guy. People misunderstood him. They thought he was a comedian. He wasn't a comedian. He was a tough guy.

HANK BAUER:

I don't think DiMaggio cared too much for him.

One game, he moved Joe to first base, trying to save his legs. He put me in center field. That was in the old Washington ballpark, where they didn't have good grass.

Joe played that game and had about sixteen chances. He was wringing wet after that ball game. He was nervous.

I sprained my ankle that day. Joe came to me later on and said, "Boy, you did me the biggest favor anybody ever did." I got hurt, so Joe had to go back to center field.

One day, Casey took Joe out of cleanup and put Mize in cleanup. And Joe really got pissed off. He didn't say nothing to him, I don't think. But you could see he was pissed.

---

*Casey could be tough on top talent. Esteemed sports journalist **ED LINN**, writing in* The Saturday Evening Post *in 1965:*

Stengel handled Mantle by turning his back on him. When he spoke about him to the press, in the later years, it was usually to criticize him. The most puzzling incident came in the course of the luncheon that was held to announce Stengel's final two-year contract with the Yankees. To Casey, it was a fitting occasion to list the greatest players of his ten-year tenure. DiMaggio was the obligatory choice as the all-time champion, of course, but from there Stengel went on to name almost every Yankee who had ever made an All-Star team—except Mickey Mantle.[2]

Casey's players were often ticked, steamed, angry, peeved, hurt, offended, and furious. The New York Journal-American *found an unidentified player who said, "I wouldn't let him in my house. I wouldn't want my wife and children to meet him."[3] So sometimes he made them mad. Sometimes that was the whole idea.* **BOBBY RICHARDSON:**

He used to describe me by saying, "He doesn't drink. He doesn't smoke. And he still can't hit .250."

It was difficult to play for him. For instance, one time he pinch-hit for me in the first inning. I remember coming back and saying, "Well, why did you start me?"

His response to that as I walked on into the clubhouse—he followed me in—he said, "You get your little mitt and go out to the bullpen and warm up Ryne Duren."

I think the way he'd bring the most out of a player was to criticize you to the press. You'd read the newspaper and read you couldn't go to your left, you couldn't do this. When you'd read that in the newspaper, it would be an embarrassment.

It would make you so mad, you'd want to go out and prove him wrong. I didn't like the way he managed, but he certainly had results.

Even though I was a young player, he gave me a chance to play. He was good with young players like that. He wanted to give them a chance. But I guess what I'm saying is that his style of management would rub older players the wrong way.

But a young player like myself, I'd just want to go out and prove him wrong.

I wasn't sure he ever learned my name. He called me "Kid." And yet, as a young player, he picked me for the All-Star team in 1959.

LEONARD KOPPETT *of* **The New York Times:**

He had a bias for the aggressive type of man, and considering the nature of his business—professional competitive athletics—it was a pretty reasonable bias. He believed that a man could be driven by abuse or other means into a quiet rage that made him a more effective player. This wasn't always true, but the record indicates it was more often true than not.[4]

<hr />

Jerry Coleman:

I'm not saying he was a charming person. He was not a warm manager with his players.

The only two guys I think he truly loved were Berra and Mantle. He loved Mickey. But he pulled him out of the game one day when he didn't run to first base. He yanked him right on the spot. Mickey would kick water coolers and such. I know—I know in my mind—that Mantle was the player that Stengel always wanted to be.

I used to get angry with Casey. One year, when Rizzuto, Willie Miranda, and I were having bad years, if you started, you were gone in the third inning. Then the next guy would come in. Then the next guy. He'd use pinch-hitters for the guys with the weak bats.

One day, Willie did something—he didn't cover the bag or something, or didn't make the play at short—a non-macho play, let me put it that way. Casey took him out in the first inning. He would do that.

In the 1950 World Series, (Whitey) Ford was pitching a shutout or something, and somebody hit a ball to Woodling and he misjudged it. This is the World Series. Stengel jumped up out of the dugout and onto the field and pushed him back with his hands.

I used to get angry with Casey. I remember we won ten in a row, eleven in a row, and he benched me the next day. I got ticked off. We all did at times.

But looking back, that's a young man, looking to get into the lineup and do the best that he can.

Reflecting as an adult, a senior citizen so to speak, you realize that he was right.

Not an uncommon sentiment. **MOOSE SKOWRON:**

Hank used to get angry. Later Hank told me he realized that Casey's platooning kept him in the big leagues longer. Right?

HANK BAUER:

I told Gene years later, "You know, he might have done us a favor. We had that damn platoon system. We both probably lasted longer than we were supposed to."

I played until I was thirty-nine, and Gene played into his forties.

DARIO LODIGIANI, *San Francisco native, major-league infielder with the Philadelphia Athletics and Chicago White Sox:*

I knew Joe DiMaggio, you know. We grew up together in North Beach in San Francisco. We went to school together.

After Joe retired, he would come up to Napa where we lived and we would have lunch. We'd talk about when we were kids and all.

I asked him one time, "When you first heard that Casey Stengel was going to be the manager of the Yankees, what did you think?"

He said, "Oh, crud. I wondered what they were doing, getting some clown to run the club."

Then he said that about halfway through the first season, Casey changed Joe's mind. He thought he handled the job and handled the pitching great. Joe respected him afterward.

As the season progressed, he won Joe DiMaggio over.

Angry with him or not, many of them craved his approval. BAUER:

One year, we had already won the pennant in September. I wasn't playing, so I was way down by the water cooler. Casey was having a meeting with the press, the New York press, at the other end of the dugout.

I heard Casey say, "Aww, he's pissed again. He can't hit right-handers." He was talking about me.

And I walked right into the middle of that meeting and I said, "Why don't you knock off that shit?"

He gave me a big wink.

You know, he treated me good after a while. Later on, after I'd been with him about four years, I played against everybody. And whenever we had an important series, we both played, no matter who the hell was pitching.

One time, one writer asked him, "Who were the best three ballplayers you managed?"

He said, "DiMaggio, Berra, and Bauer."

I said, "Me? What the hell about Mantle and those guys?" Casey said, "No. You. You gave 110 percent every time you were in the lineup."

MEL DUEZABOU, *outfielder for Casey's Oakland Oaks:*

Billy Martin was my roommate in 1948. We were very, very close. In 1956, Billy was with the Yankees and he invited me up to stay with him in New York. I remember during one of the games I was sitting up in the stands.

Billy told Casey I was up in the stands there.

Casey says, "Where? Tell the cop to bring him down."

So the cop brought me down into the dugout. I'd never seen so many photographers and newspaper people; there must have been around fifty of them surrounding Casey. I'm sitting next to him in the dugout, and they all wanted to know, "Who's that guy?"

Casey made me feel ten feet tall.

He said, "This little guy here was the damnedest line-drive hitter you ever saw. He was one of the guys who helped me get back up here."

<hr>

TOMMY HOLMES:

He liked my attitude in Boston. Even though we were losing, I remember him telling Bob Quinn about me: "That kid wants to win."

I met Casey at a card show or something, I guess it must be thirty years ago. It was in the lobby of a hotel—it must have been the Waldorf or something. I hadn't seen him in a long time.

I said, "Casey, who bought me for the Braves?"

He said, "I did."

I said, "You never saw me play, Case."

He said, "Yes, I did. When you played in Newark, I was in there with the Dodgers, and I went over to watch

Casey (right) with Boston owner Bob Quinn (left) and coach George "Highpockets" Kelly. The team changed its nickname to the Bees but could not change its terrible performances.

you play. I knew you could hit the ball. I checked your averages. I knew you could play the outfield. You had a helluva arm."

I'm thinking, *How the hell did he see this?*

He said, "I didn't care whether you got two or three hits. I wanted to watch one thing, Tommy. You hit a good pitcher. That's all I wanted to see— can you hit the good pitcher? I saw you could do that, and I went right after you."

He signs a ball for me: "To my greatest leadoff hitter." Take that anyway that you want. There's a lot of them better.

He says, "When I bought you, I wanted somebody who could hit, lead off, and get on base. And not worry about this and not worry about that. And play every day."

Oh, he praised me.

Some kids, some students, could not be reached. With the 1935 Brooklyn Dodgers, in his second season as a big-league manager, Stengel received the worst jolt a mentor can get. Outfielder Len Koenecke, one of his favorite young prospects, was playing poorly and acting erratically. Stengel demoted him. Koenecke chartered a small plane to get out of town.

During the flight, a terrible brawl erupted between Koenecke and the pilot and co-pilot. (Depending on the version of the story, he either tried to take control of the plane, or he tried to get more than friendly with the pilots.) Koenecke was killed when the co-pilot smashed him on the head with a fire extinguisher: **ROD DEDEAUX:**

Koenecke was a very likable guy. He didn't play up to his potential, that's for sure. He had all the physical attributes. He was kind of a free spirit. I had gotten to know Koenecke some when I first came out of S.C. I liked him.

Casey had to send him down because he wasn't producing. I think Casey really had high hopes for him. He'd given him every possible chance. Casey kept him in there; he was very patient. Casey was a good teacher. He knew sometimes it takes people a little longer to learn. Casey was sticking with him. But Casey had to send him down.

I had been farmed out. I was recalled, and I joined the club in Saint Louie. When I was coming into the Chase Hotel in Saint Louie to join the club, I was the happiest guy in the world. Here was a guy leaving, with his bags packed. It made me feel so badly. It hadn't occurred to me before then that if somebody is called up, somebody is leaving. It was quite a bit of a shock. I said goodbye to him on the steps. It was on that trip on the way home that he died.

It was quite a blow. He was a popular guy. Everybody was very grief-stricken. Casey was one of them.

Some didn't want to be reached, some did. **BOB SALES:**

They brought Jesse Owens into camp one year to teach people how to run. Of course, Casey did his seminar around the bases and it was just great. His thinking was that if you could get people to succeed at something, they'll think it's fun and they'll want to do it more. It was very cogent and very clear.

And some of the players looked at him like he was nuts. The older players, like Warren Spahn, they didn't like the whole idea of Casey. They thought they were big-league players. We're wearing this uniform. Who is he to tell us?

Richie Ashburn understood. He was a very astute guy about Casey. So was Roger Craig.

The whole genius of Casey and the Mets was, he deflected attention away from the players. He made them folk heroes. Marv Throneberry, for instance. He was afraid that Casey was destroying his career. Casey *made* his career. He made him into a folk hero.

I was there one day, and Marv was smoking three packs of cigarettes a day and complaining to Richie Ashburn that Casey was turning him into a joke.

Richie Ashburn said, "Relax—don't you understand what he's doing?"

There were plenty of bad-boy students. **CLIF KEANE,** *who covered Stengel's Braves for the* Boston Globe:

We had a great shortstop when Stengel had the Braves. Eddie Miller. He and Stengel didn't get along.

One day Stengel said something to Miller about playing shortstop. Miller threw the glove at him and said, "Here, you go play it, you old fart."

———◆———

Stengel knew that some of them needed tough love.
ART JOHNSON:

I remember one day, Eddie Miller, the shortstop, made some kind of a mistake. He threw to the wrong base or something. He came in, and Casey said to Miller, "That's going to cost you twenty-five dollars."

Eddie Miller said, "Make it fifty."

Casey said, "Okay, I'll make it fifty."

Eddie Miller said, "Why don't you make it seventy-five?"

And they finally went up to a hundred dollars, and finally Eddie Miller quit.

He figured he wasn't going to get the best of Casey.

———◆———

Some needed gentle, firm reminders of who was boss. **TOMMY BYRNE:**

The other team has got the bases loaded. It's two outs in the ninth. I'm pitching to a guy named Zernial, Gus Zernial. And I got him out three times, but he hit a ball to left-center pretty good. DiMaggio or somebody caught it. I had pitched a pretty good ball game. It was something like 6–3 at this point.

Casey comes out there to take me out. And I don't particularly like it. I walked away from the mound, toward short, and he's standing up on the mound. Coleman and

Yogi are standing out there. I'm not paying any attention to them. I'm letting 'em do their thing.

I looked out there at right field, and I saw who he was bringing in, a guy named Fred Sanford. Fred was a big, right-handed kid, and he could throw pretty good. He had a good curve.

I waited until he walked to within twenty-five to thirty feet of the infield. Then I walked up on the mound and I threw the ball up in the air toward right field. This Sanford, he's walking and he catches it right there at his jockstrap, so to speak. At his belt buckle.

I said, "Casey, did you see that? That was a strike."

And I walked off the mound. He really had the red-ass at me then.

He didn't do or say anything. He waited for the pitcher to get there. He gave him some instructions. But this guy, Zernial, turned around and hit a home run.

I was in the dugout and I still had the red-ass. I was there, at Casey's spot. There was a hook up there for Number 37 to hang up his jacket and so forth. I was sitting in his place. He came in and saw me sitting there, and he walked down toward the water cooler.

It wasn't long before the guy hits the ball out of the ballpark. I go into the clubhouse, sit there, and drink a beer. Pull off my shoes and stuff. We lose and everybody comes in the clubhouse.

Casey comes through part of the clubhouse and into his office. Hangs his cap up. I'd say in about a minute and a half, he comes out and he tells Pete Sheehy, the clubhouse man, to get everybody out of the back out there where the showers are. Casey has got something to say.

They all come on in there. When he sees everybody's in there, Casey says, "Next time when I go out to the mound and take a pitcher out, the pitcher and I will walk in together."

What happened was, when I came into the dugout, the crowd applauded. When Casey came in after putting in Sanford, they booed.

So he said, "From now on, we walk in together."

⸻

Some needed a kick in the butt. **RON SWOBODA:**

This was my rookie year. Stengel had pinch-hit me the first day of the season against Don Drysdale. I thought I'd have a heart attack. I ended up lining out to second base on a slider. But it was the best out I ever made, because I left with some dignity. And I got to play. I end up hitting a few home runs and I'm in the lineup.

So I'm playing in Saint Louis before the end of the first half of the season. It's a rainy day, and they put the tarp on and off the field, it must have been three times. It was one of those days. A long day of baseball.

We had a 3–0 lead. I'm in right field. The sun comes out. And the sun is going down behind third base, and I don't have sunglasses on. It's been a cloudy day, but the sun broke through.

We're in the bottom of the ninth inning. The bases are loaded. Two outs. Dal Maxvill is the hitter. Maxvill hits this little flare into short right-center—that I'm gonna catch, right? Except, as I get to the ball, the ball goes in the sun. I lose the ball. The ball gets by me, and they score all three runs.

So essentially because of my stupidity in not getting glasses, I've lost the ball game. Well, it's tied anyway.

Well, we go to bat in the top of the tenth inning. I hit

a popup to right center and I'm out. And I'm really upset. I had my helmet—these were the old fiberglass helmets; you can damage them. The helmet was sitting, open-end up, on the top step of the dugout.

I'm fuming because I didn't hit the home run that helped us win. And now we make three outs to end the top of the tenth inning. And I'm running up the steps to go out to right field, and I see this helmet there. I take my left foot and I rear up and I was just going to stomp this helmet.

Well, when I stomped it, it kind of cracked a little bit and my foot went down into it. There was enough of the helmet there that it kind of caught on my foot. So now I've got this helmet stuck on my foot, and I'm trying to shake it off.

Stengel sees this whole scene. I swear, he came up the steps like he was twenty years old. He bounded up those steps. He had this big plaster cast on his hand, because he had broken his wrist. I'm thinking he's going to crack me right on the top of the head with this plaster cast. And he grabs me by the shirt right on the top step of the dugout.

"Godammit," he said. "When you missed that fly ball, I didn't go in the locker room and throw your watch on the floor. So when you pop up and make out, I don't want you bustin' up this team's equipment."

And he took me out of the game. He jerked me right out of the game. I went down into the locker room, and I sat down and cried. I was so upset that I had screwed up the game. And so upset that Stengel had jerked me out of it.

We lose the game. Bill White hits a home run, and we lose the damn ball game.

RON HUNT:

If there was a player and Casey was chewing on his ass for any reason, it would seem to me that they were the one having a problem, not Casey. He was around that many years for a reason.

If there was somebody who was around the same number of years as him, and they had a little personality conflict, well then, that would be somebody you could listen to.

I'd say it depends on what they did. You piss Casey off, he'd bury your ass. The boss is the boss. Whether you like it or not, they're the boss.

If I didn't hustle, you're damn right I expected him to chew my ass.

Some needed to be expelled. RON SWOBODA:

Duke Carmel was a journeyman ballplayer, and he was a New York kid. This was in '64.

In spring training in Florida, we went on an east coast swing over to West Palm Beach, where Mrs. Joan Payson, the family that owned the team, had this big estate. They would throw a big steak dinner for the team.

We had this big steak dinner. These big, juicy New York cut steaks. And Lancer's. Remember that Lancer's wine? Lancer's rosé, all over the table. There was a lot of Lancer's rosé consumed.

Casey gets up to the microphone and he's going to give us a little talk. He's entertaining as hell. In between laughs and stuff, there was good, solid information there.

He said, "Look, you can't live off the money you make

as a ballplayer right now. You can't spend it as if this is money you're going to make for the rest of your life. You need to put money away, buy some annuities. So you have something to fall back on."

Then, the other thing he talked about was, "You know, when you guys go out after a ball game, don't go out with five or six guys. Everybody buys a round, and by the time you buy back, you're drunk. And it's late. If you go out with one or two guys, that makes more sense."

We're laughing because it's funny. But it's practical. And it's true.

Well, in the middle of this story, Duke Carmel—you hear his voice; he's got this New Yawk voice, like dis. He's probably had a little bit of rosé. In the midst of Casey's story, he goes, "I seen you out with ten guys."

Well, everybody hears it, and nobody quite knew how to react. But the room went kind of quiet, and Stengel got like stone-faced.

And he said, "I'll tell you something, Mr. Carmel. I've seen you when you didn't see me, either. And you haven't made this baseball team yet."

That was about all he said to him.

You talk about a cold, wet towel being thrown on the evening. Everybody knew something bad had just happened. And they were all glad that it hadn't happened to them.

The next day when we got back to Saint Petersburg, Carmel's locker was empty. He went to the minor leagues and he never saw the big leagues with the New York Mets. He would have made the team that spring.

The moral of the story is, you forget. But Stengel grew up in a rough era. Those guys were tough. You don't show him up. You can do a lot of things, but you don't show him up. Duke Carmel kind of showed him up in front of everybody.

You saw some of the rough edge there. Casey didn't take any shit.

<hr/>

Some listened to the lectures and heard nothing.
EDDIE JOOST:

He would just sit there and never really talk to anybody. He would just show up, and he'd hold meetings. He'd hold meetings, and even in those days, you just couldn't listen anymore. He'd talk Stengelese. Holy mackerel! And I finally got tired of it.

This was in the old Boston clubhouse. We had big lockers. I just put my chair in my locker, turned around, and started reading the newspaper.

He came up to me and said, "What's this?"

I said, "I'm tired of listening to all this crap. I don't know what you've said, and you've been talking for twenty minutes. You haven't said a word to me. I don't think it's fair that you hold a meeting and all you do is talk this language that you have. No one knows what the hell you're talking about."

That's the way I felt. Don't misunderstand. I wasn't playing well—I think I had the worst season of any player in the American or National League that year. I blame myself.

So this particular day, I was playing third. It was the fifth or sixth inning. We were behind by three runs. A man on first base and two outs. I'm looking at (Tony) Cuccinello, the third-base coach, figuring maybe they'd hit and run. I'm looking and he gives me the bunt sign.

So I backed up and I looked again. Same sign. I'm think-ing, *What the hell is going on? Two outs and the bunt sign?*

But I got it the second time and I thought, *Well, they want me to bunt. I don't know what the hell for. But I'll bunt.*

I did. I got thrown out and the inning's over.

Stengel screamed and yelled and ranted at me.

I said, "Wait a minute. I know that Cooch gave me the bunt sign. I got it twice, backed off, and got it again. I couldn't figure it out, but godammit, you did it. Somebody did it."

He said, "Don't talk to me like that."

I said, "Case, somebody gave the sign."

He walked away from me.

In the clubhouse after, I said to Cooch, "You know me real well. What the hell is going on?"

"Whaddya mean?"

I said, "Well, why did you give me the bunt sign with two outs? And we were behind a couple of runs."

He said, "I've got to tell you something. Case changed the signs and told me not to tell you."

He did it because I gave him a bad time down there. I had confronted him, and he didn't like the confrontation.

⋯⬥⋯

Most say he was a player's manager. Stengel looked out for his boys. **ROD KANEHL:**

I was in spring training 1959 and I was holding out. I went down unsigned, which was unheard of. You've got to be signed to go to camp with the Yankees. They didn't realize I hadn't signed.

I carpooled with Bobby Shantz, Ralph Houk, and Gil McDougald. Houk was a coach then, and they learned that

I was unsigned. Coming in one day, Houk said, "Rod, you know you're unsigned. You have to sign this Richmond contract. It has to be done."

He said, "What are you asking for?"

I told him what I was asking for.

He said, "Well, I'll relay that to Casey."

The next day, Houk came to me and said, "Don't sign until you get what you want."

Now, that's pretty powerful, isn't it? Coming from Casey. "Don't sign until you get what you want."

The next day, a guy named Jack White—he was the general manager of Richmond—said, "Let's go in here in the equipment room. We have to get you signed to a contract."

He offered me the old contract. I just looked at him and smirked.

He said, "Godammit, that Casey is in your corner."

And he had the other contract already drawn up for what I was asking for.

There is always a teacher's pet. **BOBBY BROWN:**

I think his favorite by far was Billy Martin. He just loved Martin. We used to joke that maybe he was Casey's illegitimate son or something.

DARIO LODIGIANI, *who played for Stengel's Oakland Oaks:*

Billy Martin. He was a nineteen-year-old kid. He and Casey would be arguing and yelling at one another all the time.

Casey loved that.

Billy was like his boy. They'd be shouting at one

another, and first thing you know, they'd have their arms around one another.

Chuck Symonds, Oakland Oaks batboy:

I guess the biggest thing I remember about Casey was the way he tutored Billy Martin. They moved the clubhouse in '46 from center field. Casey built this special dressing room for the batboys and ballboys. Billy Martin was in high school then, trying out, because he was a friend of the trainer's. Billy dressed with us. I got to know Billy pretty well.

Casey really took a liking to Billy's fiery attitude. He just really worked with him, all the time. Ground balls, ground balls. Talked to him. He really took him under his wing.

That's why when Billy went to the Yankees, he took uniform Number 1. Because Casey wore Number 1 with Oakland.

In 1957, the Stengel-Martin relationship was fractured when Martin was traded from the Yankees to the lowly Kansas City Athletics. Martin was devastated and didn't speak to Casey for years. **Bobby Richardson:**

We played a ball game in Kansas City. We were out on the bus after the game; Billy Martin and Stengel stayed in the clubhouse. We waited for about forty-five minutes. And when they did come out, there was an empty seat by me.

Billy sat down by me and said, "Okay, kid. It's all yours. I've been traded to Kansas City."

He loved the Yankees and hated to leave.

Martin came home in the 1970s. **BOB CASE:**

When he was managing the Texas Rangers, Billy wrote Casey a letter, on Texas Rangers stationery. I read the letter. He wanted to bury the hatchet.

When Casey died, I went down to LAX to pick up Martin when he flew in from Texas. It was on a Sunday night.

They had the wake at the house. The funeral was at Forest Lawn. When I picked Martin up at the airport, he said, "Can you drive me by the mortuary?" He wanted to see Casey.

I drove him to the mortuary and waited in the lobby there. Billy said, "I'll be right out."

About a half-hour goes by. There's nobody there—it's a Sunday night. I wonder what the hell is he doing? So I walk in there, and Billy was sobbing over Casey's corpse.

I said, "Billy, we've got to go."

He was just sobbing, sobbing. And he actually kissed Casey's corpse. I pulled him away and we exited the place.

On the night before the funeral, Billy Martin slept in Casey Stengel's bed.

Mets scout **HARRY MINOR:**

Billy was so broke up at his funeral. Billy was just inconsolable. He went back to Casey's house there, and Billy wouldn't come out of his bedroom for an hour or two. He was just bawling like a baby.

Casey was like a father to him.

3

$$\Longrightarrow$$

CLASS CLOWNS

Fifty-seven years I'm in this business, you learn a few things. . . . Words with a "K" in it are funny. . . . Cupcake is funny. Tomato is not funny. . . . Casey Stengel, that's a funny name. Robert Taylor is not funny.

— Willie, veteran vaudevillian
in Neil Simon's *The Sunshine Boys*

Chat up old ballplayers about Joe DiMaggio, and in the course of the conversation there will be soft talk of mystery and respect. The man was so complicated.

Talk to old ballplayers about Ted Williams, and they will shake their head in awe at his dedication and obsession. The man pursued baseball perfection the way John Hinckley pursued Jodie Foster.

Talk to old ballplayers about Casey Stengel, and there will be respect and awe and . . . giggles. The man was a riot.

Almost everyone ended up giggling.

Al Lopez giggled.

Ralph Houk giggled.

Ron Swoboda sometimes couldn't stop giggling.

Casey Stengel daydreamed in his youth about a career in vaudeville, and he never quite let go of the dream. Throughout his baseball career and into old age, he was a humorist. He did standup monologues. He did physical comedy. He did knife-to-the-heart one-liners.

He liked words and language. You never knew what he was going to say next. But you had to chuckle at a man who would uncork, right there in public, utterances such as the time he was signing autographs and he said, "Give 'em here. I'll sign anything but veal cutlets. My ballpoint pen slips on cutlets."[1]

A typical jokester, Stengel used humor the way some people use a Swiss army knife. For many, many purposes.

Sometimes he used it to defend himself. Such as the famous day he returned to Brooklyn with the Pirates. The Flatbush fans razzed him, and he hid a sparrow under his hat, so when Stengel tipped his cap, the bird flew out. The crowd cheered him.

Often he used it to make a point. Like the time he stood in right field at Ebbets Field, theatrically slashing his contract with a pair of scissors to dramatize his latest pay cut.

Or the many times as a manager when he pretended to faint dead away at the absurdity of an umpire's call.

Which worked pretty well until the day umpire Beans Reardon pretended to faint right alongside him. "When I peeked out of one eye and saw Reardon lying on the ground, too, I knew I was licked," Casey said. "So I got up and walked away."

Or the time with the Pirates when he was thrown out of a game by umpire Pete Harrison for arguing a decision. Stengel received a telegram telling him he was fined twenty-five dollars.

Stengel pinned the telegram to his uniform whenever he stepped to the plate and Harrison was umpiring. "See this?" Stengel said. "You made a mistake, but it cost me twenty-five bucks."

Sometimes he used it to vent frustration and inflict some damage. Like when his Mets kept losing and losing, and he said, "The only thing worse than a Mets game is a Mets doubleheader."

Most often Casey used humor because it kept his players relaxed.

Tra-la-la.

"He was a comedian guy," said Dario Lodigiani, who played infield for Stengel's Oakland Oaks. "He'd tell us stories and act up in a lot of ways. He'd tell us about his experiences when he had Brooklyn and the Boston Braves—bad clubs—about how he got fired and all. He kept us all loose. That was his style of managing."

Besides, it was just plain fun to hoot around.

Like the time he arranged to have a grapefruit dropped out of an airplane on Uncle Wilbert Robinson. Or the time he crawled into a drainage hole and disappeared in right field, popping up at the last moment to snare a fly ball.

And like every time he broke into Stengelese, the famous gibberish that he poured over everyone from John McGraw to Estes Kefauver.

Stengel was a funny man, and he attracted other funny people. And somehow he often found himself in absurd, ridiculous situations, such as at the helm of the 1935 Brooklyn Dodgers and the 1962 New York Mets.

But he found humor everywhere, even with the stuffy Yankees.

"He made a comment once about my wife and I riding camels," said Tommy Byrne, the tough old Yankee lefty.

Byrne was beginning a story about Casey Stengel.
He was giggling.

BOB CASE, *Stengel's friend and business manager:*

You know when he broke his leg, when he was hit by the cab in Boston? All the neighbors would talk about how he used to walk backwards through the neighborhood after that.

He did the same thing after he broke his hip. You'd see Casey walking around the neighborhood backwards.

People loved him. They thought he was kind of crazy.

They'd tell stories about him. They had a huge flood in the '20s in Glendale. All the neighbors said his house was flooded.

Casey was just sitting out on his balcony with an umbrella, listening to the radio. The bottom half of his house was underwater.

MAX WEST:

We were playing in Cincinnati. We had the first-base dugout. You had to go through the stands and go over behind the stands on the third-base side, and they had a house that they made into a clubhouse. That's where we dressed.

This happened to be on a Sunday. The umpire at third base was Lou Jorda. We were ahead. In right field, they had a little cement wall, oh, about two feet high. And it might have been six feet thick. On top of that, they had a chain-link fence on pipe. The whole thing wasn't more than six feet tall.

So anyway, Ival Goodman hit a line drive out there to me. I turned around to get it off the fence. It happened to hit the edge of that cement and bounce right back into my glove. Bang. Real quick, right into my glove.

I turned around and threw him out at second base.

The umpire was circling his hand to signal home run.

Casey (right) with Saint Louis Browns manager Fred Haney. They might be discussing the ins and outs of managing awful ball clubs.

Well, first of all, nobody out in the bleachers moved. Which they normally would if a ball went in there. It wasn't a home run.

Stengel comes running out of there. He's arguing with him and stuff. I just sort of walked down there to listen to Stengel argue with Lou Jorda and the first-base umpire. Just listening. I didn't get into the argument at all.

Stengel is arguing with him. The fans knew it, and they were screaming on our side. Eventually, they were throwing bottles. It almost started a riot.

They finally threw Stengel out of the ball game.

He went over to that clubhouse that was in a house. He went into the shower and he was in there, all lathered up.

In the meantime, the umpire said to me, "Don't you say anything."

I said, "If you hadn't made such a big mistake, we wouldn't be in this mess."

And he threw me out of the game. I think that was the first time I got thrown out of a game anywhere.

So I go over to the clubhouse. I'm walking in, and I look in there and Casey is taking a shower.

He says, "What happened to you?"

I said, "Well, he threw me out of the game, too."

Casey said, "That SOB!"

And he ran right out of there and started to run right out the front door. Naked, with soap all over him. And I had to stop him at the front door.

I yelled at him, "Case! You don't have any clothes on! Stop!"

I grabbed him by the arm.

All he had on him was lather. He was headed out the door.

——— ◆ ———

JACK LANG, *who covered Stengel's Mets for the* **Long Island Press:**

He had a reputation as a clown, and he didn't do anything to deny it. Baseball to him was fun.

The Mets had a pitcher who had gone to Yale, Ken MacKenzie, a left-handed pitcher they got from Milwaukee. He was a relief pitcher. Casey brought him into the game one day.

Casey handed him the ball, after the long trip out from the bullpen, and said, "Make out like it's the Harvards."

When the Mets were so bad, he said, "Maybe we can trade one of them to every team and we can bring them down to our level."

In '62, the Mets had an outfielder by the name of Frank Thomas. He led the club in home runs. He was a great pull hitter.

There was a sign on a billboard out in left field, from King Korn stamps, and the Met who hit the sign the most times during the year was going to get a boat.

Thomas was always pulling balls down the left-field line. He hit a lot of home runs that way at the Polo Grounds.

Stengel wanted him to go the other way one day. Stengel yelled at him, "If you want a boat, join the navy!"

SAM SUPLIZIO, *Yankees minor-league outfielder in the 1950s:*

Remember Bruce Swango? He's the bonus baby who some scout warmed up in a garage or something. The ball made such a popping sound because they were in this garage or barn, and the scout said, "Listen to that. This guy is faster than (Bob) Feller! You should hear the mitt pop!"

Well, anyway, Baltimore signed him and he was all over the place. He couldn't even pitch batting practice. So Bruce Swango was history, real quick.

But he could hit a little bit, so the Yankees picked him up. We had him in spring training.

So we're going down the sliding pits. Stengel is teaching us how to slide. We're all sliding as hard as we can in the sand. We're doing the best job to show off. We're busting our ass.

Here comes Swango. He's an outfielder now. Swango goes clomp-clomp. He's just running on flat feet, just stomping, running down to slide. He leaps into his slide and he comes down on both feet.

He looks up. Casey had the rake. After each kid slid, Casey raked it level.

Swango said, almost crying, "Mr. Stengel, I can't slide. I've been a pitcher all my life and I can't slide. How about if I rake the pit?"

Casey says, "You're my assistant. Here's the rake."

⚬──⟨═⟩──⚬

RON SWOBODA:

I was in the car the other day with Ralph Kiner, and he was telling a couple of Casey stories.

After that first year, when (the Mets) lost 120 games, they lost a particularly terrible game the last day of the season, to end up with that terrible record.

Coming off the field after that last game, Casey allegedly said, "Fellas, just remember. It was a team effort."

And one time when they lost one in extra innings. Casey said to the writers, "We're getting better. It's taking them longer to beat us."

⚬──⟨═⟩──⚬

He wasn't above old tricks. RUGGER ARDIZOIA, who pitched for Stengel's 1946 Oakland Oaks:

We used to have the first car after the baggage car. He had a good one for rookie guys, pitchers who would come on the ball club.

On the Pullmans, they had double-deckers, you know? Lower and upper. In the upper berth they had a sling for your clothes and stuff. He used to tell the pitchers to go up there and rest their arm in the sling so the pitching arm would be rested.

RAY BERRES, *catcher for Stengel on the Brooklyn Dodgers in 1934, on how pitcher Walter Beck acquired the nickname "Boom-boom":*

That was the story in Philadelphia, the old bandbox. I was there. It was a hot, humid day.

Beck was the pitcher. They started hitting him pretty good. They started hitting the ball off the wall. Hack Wilson was playing right field. He'd have to keep retrieving that ball off the wall and hustle back in.

So Casey went out to talk to Walter. While Casey was doing that, Hack went and leaned on the right field wall along the box seats.

Beck got mad. He was disgusted with himself. He turned around and threw that ball off the fence.

Boom! Off that tin wall.

Hack was just leaning up against that fence, not paying attention to what was going on out on the pitcher's mound. Hack heard the crash, ran like hell to the ball, and wheeled it on into second base.

When Hack found out he had made a mistake, he felt as silly as hell.

Casey said to Boom-boom Beck later on, "If you had thrown it that hard at the hitter, you would still be in there."

GALEN CISCO:

I remember one time at the Polo Grounds, we had a rain delay. I guess Casey was a pretty good friend of Buddy Hackett.

During the rain delay, Buddy Hackett came into the clubhouse and entertained us for about a half-hour. He went on and on.

That gives you kind of an idea what kind of a guy Casey was—to bring us Buddy Hackett to entertain us.

BOB SALES:

There was one year when he called everybody "doctor." I think he had probably been in a hospital. He always screwed up names anyway.

I think he must have been in a hospital in the off-season, and saw that everybody was being called doctor. So he thought that was a terrific name for everybody, because he couldn't remember names. He called everybody doctor for months.

HANK BAUER:

He didn't know a lot of names. He'd just call, "Hey, you."

One day Gene was playing left field in Yankee Stadium. I wasn't playing and I was way down by the water cooler. In the top of the eighth, Casey was looking for a pinch-hitter for the bottom of the eighth.

Casey hollered down, "Hey, Woodling. Get a bat."

Nobody moved or anything.

"Hey, Woodling. Get a bat."

Pretty soon he came up in front of me and said, "Godammit, I said get a bat!"

I said, "Godammit, Woodling's playing left field. My name's Bauer."

JACK LANG:

He had strange names for people. He couldn't remember people's names. He knew who they were, but he didn't always remember their names.

One time, he called down to the bullpen. Joe Pignatano was down there. Casey said, "Tell Nelson to get up."

Pignatano knew the Mets didn't have anyone named Nelson, but he didn't want to argue with him. Another time, he had said something and the old man got him back with a sharp remark or something.

Pignatano just took the ball and put it on the rubber in the bullpen and said, "He wants Nelson."

Up got Bob Miller, who said, "That's me. That's what he always calls me. Nelson."

ROD KANEHL:

He used to call me "Canoe."

GALEN CISCO:

He couldn't keep names straight. He always called me "Ohio State." I went to school there. For some reason, he associated with that. Once in a while he'd call me by name. But he called me Ohio State a lot.

We had two Millers on the team. He called down to the bullpen one afternoon. Sheriff Robinson was the coach. Casey told Sheriff, "Call down there and get Miller up."

Sheriff called down on the phone and said, "Get Miller up."

He said, "Which one do you want? We got two here."

And he said, "Hey, Casey. Which Miller do you want?"

Casey said, "Just surprise me."

MAX WEST:

We were playing at the Polo Grounds. Late in the season, that Coogan's Bluff was behind you. About the sixth inning or the seventh inning, it would get pretty dark. We didn't have lights. The umpire was Beans Reardon. He lived in Long Beach. Casey and Beans were good friends. They used to go to the races at Santa Anita and so forth.

Both of them liked to talk. Beans never shut up.

So we were playing at the Polo Grounds, and we were about four or five runs ahead. It got dark.

So Stengel went out to Beans and wanted him to call the game because of the dark. He didn't want anyone to get hurt. And of course, he argued for it more than normal because we were ahead.

So anyway, he's yelling at him to call the game. They get into a big argument. The game didn't mean that much now. Now the important thing was the argument about whether to call the game or not.

I don't know where he came up with these things, but Casey came out with a couple of big flashlights.

He walks from the dugout to about halfway to home plate and he's yelling, "Two flashes for Posedel! Three flashes for Sullivan!" He's signaling to the bullpen.

Then he's going around trying to find home plate with these flashlights.

Naturally, Beans had to kick him out of the game. The next day, the commissioner called him. I suppose he fined him.

⸺⊰⊱⸺

HANK BAUER:

Yogi Berra was up there hitting in Yankee Stadium. He's a bad-ball hitter, you know, and he swung at a real bad ball. And Casey yelled out, "Godammit, do a little thinking out there."

Yogi turned around and yelled at him, "How the hell do you think and hit at the same time?"

⸺⊰⊱⸺

BOBBY BROWN, the Yankees infielder and medical doctor:

When I met him that first spring training, he told me that we had something in common. He said he was a professional man, too.

I said, "What do you mean by that?"

He said that he took a correspondence course in dentistry.

I said, "Really? Did you ever practice?"

He said he couldn't because they didn't make left-handed tools in those days.

⸺⊰⊱⸺

MAX WEST:

The clubhouse in Braves Field was a huge, big barn. This was after the cab hit him and broke his leg in Kenmore

Square. He had broken his leg, and they had taken the cast off it and he's walking around without any pants on.

Al Lopez looked at him and said, "Casey—what happened to your shin?"

Casey said, "The goddamn doctor put my leg on backwards."

<hr />

ROD DEDEAUX:

He had a character playing for him by the name of Frenchy Bordagaray. I joined the Dodgers right out of college, reported right to them. Casey, possibly thinking that Bordagaray and I were both French, thought I might have some sobering influence on him. So he was my roommate.

Frenchy was quite a character. He had great ability, but he was a character. Casey handed him the lineup one day to take to the umpire. Frenchy wasn't playing at the time; he wasn't a regular. So he erased the name at the top and put himself down as the leadoff man.

We were visiting. I'll always remember Frenchy going up to bat. Casey turns around and sees Frenchy at the plate, and he damn near went crazy. He went out to see what the hell was going on.

He went out and said somebody else was supposed to be up. The umpire pulled out the lineup card and pointed to the leadoff spot. It took a while for it to sink in with Casey that Frenchy had changed it.

But you know, those kind of things could only happen to Casey.

Oddities had a way of finding him. A woman who had stalked an American League player years before showed up on Stengel's doorstep after he retired.
HARRY MINOR, *Mets scout and Stengel friend:*

She was weird. When she was involved with the player, it was like *The Natural.* No matter what he did, he looked up and she'd be staring at him. She used to write letters to him, ten pages long.

She came out and misled Casey. She said the Mets had sent her. To take care of him. Of course, we hadn't.

I took Casey to the doctor one day. As far as I knew, she was taking care of him. We went to the doctor and Casey went back in the room. And this gal, she wouldn't let Casey go anywhere without her. She was sitting there, and after a while the doctor came out and said, "Mr. Minor, could I see you for a moment?" And she got up to go back with me, and he said, "No, just Mr. Minor."

So the doctor took me back to the room. Casey is sitting there on the table, dangling his feet over the edge, and he said, *"Get that woman out of here!"*

She was driving him crazy.

ROD DEDEAUX:

He liked to tell the story of when I joined the Brooklyn team. I was there a week or two, and I wasn't playing in any ball games at all. There was this breakfast, a communion breakfast with about a thousand people at a Mass. The Catholics from the team were there, Frenchy, Lopez, Cuccinello. I was Catholic and I went, too.

They got together and decided that when they needed someone to speak, I would be their spokesperson. There I was, a rookie just out of California, with a bunch of major leaguers speaking in front of a thousand people.

I said what I had to say. Casey later told me that the general manager of the club, Bob Quinn, told Casey, "I don't know whether Raoul—that's what they called me at the time—can play baseball, but I'll tell you this: He's the best speaker you ever signed."

Casey would tell that story and everyone would get a big kick out of it. He could dramatize it.

JACK LANG:

We were sitting on the bench in the Polo Grounds one day. The Mets had just acquired a catcher from the Giants, Joe Pignatano. The trade was announced like eleven o'clock in the morning. The Mets were playing a night game.

Pignatano took the train up from Philadelphia, and rather than taking the train to his home in Brooklyn, he took the subway straight to the Polo Grounds. He got there like three, four o'clock in the afternoon.

The clubhouse guy gives him a uniform, and he goes out and sits on the bench.

About five o'clock, before batting practice, out comes Stengel. He's sitting on the bench and he's starts talking to Pignatano. Back and forth, they're talking.

I got there around six o'clock, during batting practice. I knew Joe from his days with the Dodgers. I said hello to him and everything.

At the time, the Mets had about three or four catchers. I said, "Who's catching tonight, Casey?"

Casey says, "That new guy from the Giants, if he ever gets here."

He had been talking to Pignatano for about an hour on the bench.

Sometimes Casey spoke in Stengelese for fun, sometimes to dodge a question. Sometimes he couldn't help it; the words just flowed out like candy from an overstuffed piñata. He had seen a lot, and remembered everything. Sometimes it was asking too much for the stories to file out in an orderly fashion. **SIBBY SISTI:**

I was managing in the Milwaukee organization at the time, I think it was 1957, when the Braves won the pennant and they played the Yankees in the World Series. I was sitting on the bench during batting practice with Bob Holbrook, who was a sportswriter from Boston.

The Yankees were having hitting practice. Bob nudged me and said, "Lookit there."

Casey was up by the batting cage, and a lot of sportswriters were around him. There must have been eight or ten. Bob told me, "Sib, lookit those guys. When Casey gets through talking, they still won't know what the hell he was talking about."

Casey used to start one story and not finish it, and go on to another one and not finish that, and go on to a third one and not finish it. And then go back to the original story.

PHOTO COURTESY OF SAM CATANEO

Casey with promising Braves infielder Sibby Sisti. Stengel liked to pick out young players with potential, zero in on them, and teach them everything he knew.

MEL DUEZABOU:

He was very, very comical. In spring training, he would get us all sitting around when we weren't playing, in the hotel, and he would tell us different stories, about when he played. We all thought it was funnier than hell at the time. We'd sit there laughing.

He would be in the lobby of the hotel, and there would be four or five players around him. He'd get to talking, waving his arms and so forth.

Halfway through, you'd stop and say, "What the hell is he talking about?" This was actually true. The words came out of his mouth, but they didn't make sense. He had a knack for it. But he had everybody listening.

BOBBY RICHARDSON:

We traveled in those days by train. I remember being in the dining car and sitting close enough to hear him talk.

His double-talk, of course, would take you from one place to another. Eventually, he might come back to where he started out.

WILL CLONEY, who covered Stengel's Braves for the Boston Herald:

He was a very smart guy. I think his double-talk was a lot of nonsense. I think he knew just as well as you and I what he was saying.

MARK FREEMAN, who pitched for the 1959 Yankees:

I wish I had made a tape recording. I would have to hide behind the lockers when we had a clubhouse meeting. I had never heard anything like that. I have never heard anybody ramble on like that. Honestly, I would get tears in my eyes, I was laughing so much.

The old Yankees had heard it before, so they didn't think it was funny. I had to hide, I was laughing so hard.

DARIO LODIGIANI:

Stengelese. He'd get a group of people, and they'd get to talking about some of his experiences that happened. He'd cut sentences in half. Everyone would start looking at him and thinking, *What the hell is he saying?*

Then he'd walk away and leave them like that. He'd walk away!

A couple of times, I'd walk away with Casey and he would say to me, "I got 'em now."

He knew what he was doing.

BOB SALES:

There was a guy named Grover Powell. He was a left-handed pitcher. I think he went to the University of Pennsylvania. He pitched very well one day, so he was backed up against his locker, being interviewed by everybody.

Casey goes along on the outside. Casey always thought the questions were kind of weird, right? So Casey says, "Was you born in Poland?"

I think he was just making fun of the kind of questions people ask. Nobody could ever really figure out where that came from.

JERRY COLEMAN:

He used to call people "road apples." You know what road apples are, don't you? It's horse's stool. I didn't know. I had to look it up. If he didn't like you, you were a road apple.

A "plumber" was a guy who couldn't play well. "Jelly leg" was a guy who didn't have any speed. "Ned in the third(-grade) reader" was someone or something that was dumb, naïve.

You've got to go back to the turn of the century to come up with some of those things.

ROD DEDEAUX:

The Dodgers had been on a losing streak. Frenchy was violating one of the basic rules of baseball by playing catch in front of the dugout. Casey came out of the dugout, and Frenchy threw the ball and hit him right in the head. He nearly knocked him out. Casey sat down on the bench and needed to take some time to recover.

The Dodgers won that game. And the next day, Frenchy said in half-seriousness, "Hitting you worked pretty good. You want to try it again?" I'm telling you, he was half-serious.

SIBBY SISTI:

We trained in San Antonio one year. We went to Mexico and played the Browns over there. The Browns were training in San Antonio also. They had two Greyhound buses and we had one Greyhound going into Monterrey, Mexico. The people were all lined up along the street.

Casey said, "Geez, it's nice that the people come out to cheer us."

Somebody made the remark that they weren't cheering us. It was just the first time they had seen Greyhound buses.

GALEN CISCO:

I happened to be pitching this day. We were playing the Giants, and Willie McCovey was on a roll. We decided how we were going to pitch him and how we were going to defense him. We got our infielders set, the outfielders set.

Casey used to always sit in the back of the room. At the end, when we were finished with McCovey, he spoke up.

He said, "Now I forgot. Are we going to play the right fielder in the upper deck or lower deck?"

SAM SUPLIZIO:

I'm in the back dressing where the non-roster guys were, a little cubbyhole in a barracks building in Fort Lauderdale, at Miller Huggins Field. There were about five of us.

It's early morning and it's early in spring training. You know the story about Don Larsen wrapping his baby-blue Cadillac around a light pole and almost getting killed, the year after he pitched his perfect game? This was the day after that happened.

Well, I heard this. The media were in the clubhouse, and we were kind of off in the corner. But Casey talked so loud, so they asked him the question: "What do you think of your fair-haired boy now?"

Casey said, "Well, fellas, I'll tell you. That boy either goes to bed late or gets up awful early."

They just wet their pants. This guy could fend off the toughest question with the funniest remark you ever heard.

JACK LANG:

We were at the Chase Hotel in Saint Louis one night. They had a club there where they had top-name entertainment.

We were sitting just off the stage. The singer was Robert Goulet. Robert Goulet comes out and he sings, and he's into about his third or fourth song and all of a sudden he spots Stengel down at this table.

He just stopped in the middle of the song.

He said, "Oh, my God. In the audience tonight is one of the most cherished heroes in all of baseball. Casey Stengel! I wish you'd come up Mr. Stengel and take a bow."

Casey came up, and the next thing you know, he's bowing and being very cute.

All of a sudden in the conversation, he says to Robert Goulet, "Yes, I have the same effeminate appeal that you do."

MARK FREEMAN:

When we were in Saint Petersburg, we stayed at the Sorrento Hotel. There were a lot of elderly people there. Every year the hotel would give a dinner dance. All the Yankees were supposed to come there.

Casey would bring his wife, Edna. She liked to dance. I loved to dance in those days; I was a pretty good dancer. So I went over and asked Edna to dance. We danced one. She wanted to stay out there and dance another one. And dance another one.

Afterward I took her back to the table. I said, "Thank you, Casey."

He said, "Fine."

The next day he told the press, "If he could pitch half as well as he can dance, he'd win twenty games."

Chuck Symonds, *batboy for Stengel's Oakland Oaks:*

Billy Martin and Lou Stringer got into a fight when Hollywood was playing in Oakland. They got into a fight at second base. Of course, both benches cleared.

When the melee was over and Casey ran back to the Oakland dugout, he was wearing a Hollywood hat. He picked up the wrong hat. Myself and the visiting batboy, we just stood there and laughed.

Mark Freeman:

Somebody told me this one:

Yogi was staggering around under a popup behind home plate. He missed the ball and he ended up right in front of Casey in the dugout. Casey said, "What the hell, Yogi?"

Yogi says, "I lost it in the sky."

Casey says, "The sky has been there for years."

There was a guy he liked—Rod Kanehl. Rod could run and that was about it. But Casey thought he was funny.

I was on the bench in spring training when this happened: There was a guy named Danny Napoleon. He was a rookie trying out with whoever we were playing that day.

Casey yelled down the bench, "Anybody know this guy?" He wanted to know how to pitch him.

Rod Kanehl said, "Yeah, I do."

Casey said, "Well, what about him?"

Rod Kanehl said, "He can't ever get his hand out of his shirt."

Casey thought it was so funny, he gave Rod Kanehl a chance to play with the Yankees, with the Mets. And all he could do was run. And he was funny.

This is another one that was told to me: It was a windy day and there was a popup hit. I think it was Ted Williams who hit it. Real high, behind home plate. Yogi wandered around and wandered around, and the ball hit about fifteen feet to his right.

Casey yelled, "Yogi, what happened? Did it take a bad hop?"

BILL RAIMONDI, who played under Stengel with the Oakland Oaks:

I remember one time during a game, Casey wanted the pitcher to do something, but the pitcher wasn't paying any attention to him. Casey had an apple. He took the apple core and threw it at the mound. That got the pitcher's attention.

GALEN CISCO:

We were playing the Cardinals. I happened to be pitching. Do you remember the name Carl Warwick? He was kind of a no-name player. He played a few years, but he wasn't a big name.

Anyway, Casey said, "Under no circumstances throw him a fastball. No circumstances." Because he couldn't hit anything else most of the time.

I happened to be getting behind on him in this particular at-bat. I had to throw him a fastball. So I threw him a fastball and he hit it out of the ballpark. It just barely got over the fence.

Casey came out and he said, "Do you remember what we said about pitching to this guy?"

I said, "Yeah—don't throw him any fastballs is what we said. But I got behind and I had to throw something that I could get over the plate. I threw him a fastball and I don't have any excuses."

Casey turned around and he left.

In this guy's third at-bat, I threw him three straight curveballs. The third one he hit way the hell out of the ballpark. I mean, *way* out.

Out comes Casey and he said, "Now Galen, what did we say about this guy?"

I said, "Casey, that was a curveball. And yours went farther than mine."

EDDIE JOOST, of Stengel's Boston Braves:

Jim Tobin was there. He was a knuckleballer. He was a great guy. He liked to have a couple of pops now and then. He fell asleep on the bench one day. Stengel's going to make a change. Tobin's down on the end of the bench, half asleep.

Casey yells, "Tobin! Get up. Come on, get going."

Tobin jumps up and says, "Okay, whaddya want me to do? Want me to pitch?"

Stengel says, "No. Go out to the bullpen and warm up."

Tobin sits down and says, "No. Why do I need to go to the bullpen and warm up? I throw a knuckleball."

SAM SUPLIZIO:

John Malagone was the guy who was supposed to succeed Yogi Berra as the Yankees catcher. John was a boxer in the army. Funnier than hell. A big, strong kid.

He wasn't a great catcher. I played with him in Binghamton, New York.

Now we're on the field; we're all rookies. Malagone comes late. He gets out of a cab, smoking a cigar. He stands there watching us. We all look and we say, "Hey, that's Johnny. And he's late."

Stengel looked up. "That boy's late."

He goes in and changes his clothes. So we're out there busting our ass, and here comes John Malagone. John gets a bat and he's coming up to get his whacks in the batting cage.

Casey says, "Hey, boy. Did you get your shagging in?"

Malagone says, "Casey, I don't feel like shagging. I think all I want to do is hit."

The guys around the batting cage, we laugh like hell.

You know what Casey said? He said, "Son, you've got the guts to tell me that. You go in and hit. The rest of you guys get out there and shag while John hits."

HARRY MINOR, on Stengel's banquet-circuit performances:

We were introducing Roy McMillan, the old shortstop, as our manager at Visalia. John Murphy and Whitey Herzog, Dee Fondy, Casey, and myself all headed up there for this dinner.

It wasn't a big affair, but Casey got up and everything he said just came out funny. If I had made a recording of it, you could have made a lot of money on it. He was really on a roll, and he just went on and on. There were only about fifty people in this restaurant. Everybody was in hysterics, rolling on the floor.

CHUCK STEVENS, *who played first base for the Saint Louis Browns and who for many years served as secretary-treasurer of the Association of Professional Ball Players of America:*

In show business, they say that the one guy who knocked Jack Benny out was George Burns. He'd walk into a room and Jack Benny would fall off the chair. He just thought he was the funniest guy in the world.

That was the thing with Stengel. He'd start talking and I would go bonkers. I'd heard these stories a million times, but to me he was funny.

ART JOHNSON:

I remember one day sitting in the dugout and a young reporter came in. He said, "Mr. Stengel, I'm so-and-so from the *Boston Record-American*."

"Sure," Casey said.

So he asked him some questions. Casey answered them. Finally, one of them was, "Mr. Stengel, in your opinion, what do you think is the most important position on a baseball team?"

Casey said, "Well, the catcher, of course. If you don't have a catcher, every pitch goes right to the backstop."

You never expected anything else from Casey Stengel during an interview. He always had one or two lines that were funny.

⊷⊷⊷

TOMMY BYRNE:

I remember we played an armed forces team on Guam. I pitched in the rain that day. They hit a ball to left-center. I think the left fielder and the center fielder ran together and they couldn't find the ball.

They finally got it in there, and I went to slide into third base. Casey was coaching third. I slid and I landed in mud—so I came up about three feet short. And I'm lying there, wringing wet in the mud.

I'm looking up at Casey and he's looking down at me. And I said, "Say, could you bring that base over here?"

⊷⊷⊷

JACK LANG:

There was the time Marv Throneberry hit a triple. The umpire called him out for not touching first base.

Cookie Lavagetto was the first-base coach. When Casey came out of the dugout to argue with the umpire, Cookie stopped him.

He said, "Case, you better not argue too long, because he missed second base, too."

Casey said, "I know he touched third, because he's standing on it."

⊷⊷⊷

SIBBY SISTI, *on a zinger that Stengel used from the Toledo Mud Hens to the New York Mets:*

One day, we had a meeting. He was disgusted with the whole ball club. We weren't winning. He advised all of us to buy stock in the Pennsylvania and Erie Railroad.

He said, "Because there's going to be a lot of guys getting shipped out of here."

RAY BERRES, *catcher on Stengel's 1934 Brooklyn Dodgers:*

A ball was hit to Frenchy Bordagaray one day. It caromed off the wall and he retrieved it. He threw it, but instead of it going to the relay man, the second baseman, it went into the left-field corner. The left-field corner!

By the time they got the ball and threw it in, it was an inside-the-park home run.

Casey got a big kick out of everything. So when the inning was over, everybody rushed into the dugout to see what he had to say to Frenchy.

Before Casey could say a word, Frenchy said, "Now wait a minute, Case. Wait a minute. You're going to jump all over me for that play that I just made.

"But I need to tell you. You have to get somebody out there to line up the cutoff right."

ROD KANEHL:

This was in '62. We were in Dodger Stadium and it was like the first week of August. He called a meeting. He said,

"Well, you guys can relax now. We're mathematically eliminated from the pennant." And that was in the first week of August.

We relaxed. We relaxed and won seven more games for the rest of the year.

———◆———

MARK FREEMAN:

I think I was pitching against Detroit. I walked the first guy. I hit the second guy. A ground ball went to Kubek. Perfect double play. He threw it over Richardson's head at second, and it went down the right-field line. I walked another guy and had the bases loaded.

Rocky Colavito came to the plate. I had the count 2–2 on him with the bases loaded. I knew I really had to show Casey something. As I was taking my windup—in those days we did that with the bases loaded—as I got into the top of my windup, a bug flew into my eye.

I stopped and backed off the mound. It was one of those bugs that burned a lot.

Gus Mauch was the trainer. He came right out there, and he got a piece of gauze and dug it right out of my eye. He went to show it to the umpire, because the umpire had called a balk. The umpire wouldn't even look at it. I got out of the inning later. Except for that one moment, I had gone on to pitch pretty well.

The next day we were at Al Lang Field playing the Cardinals, and I was sitting next to Casey on the bench.

I said, "Casey, what do you do if a bug flies into your eye like that while you're winding up?"

He started to answer me seriously, but he noticed there were several writers listening in.

So he said, "Son, if you're going to make the Yankees, you're going to have to learn to catch that bug in your mouth."

***

It's always funny until someone loses an eye. Or someone goes too far. Was it possible to take a joke over the line with Casey Stengel? Yes. Outfielder Jim Piersall pulled it off with the 1963 Mets. **ROD KANEHL:**

Jimmy Piersall declared that when he hit his one hundredth home run, he was going to run around the bases backwards. I was thinking he was going to third to second to first. He meant he was going to turn around and run backwards.

So he does. He turns around and runs them backwards.

Now, in '62 we were bad; we lost 120 games. We got two rained out with Houston. Thank God we didn't have to make them up—40–120 sounds better than 40–122.

Anyway, this next year, we're trying hard. We're doing the best we can, and now we're clowns. See, Piersall made us clowns, a circus act, by running the bases backwards.

There were some guys from '62 who really didn't appreciate him running those bases backwards. We never did anything that wasn't baseball—until Piersall showed up. He'd be on the Johnny Carson show, he'd be joking about us. That wasn't happening before Piersall got there.

He was gone within a week. Because Casey knew that twenty-four guys were really trying, and here was a guy who was promoting himself. He would talk about Casey sleeping on the bench and so on—just to promote Jimmy Piersall.

He was gone.

Casey was a showman. He did stuff. He did the bird-out-of-the-hat. But I think maybe Piersall was infringing on Casey's territory.

4

SELECTED LECTURES

Now they say I talk around corners and talk up blind alleys, but old Case don't leave anybody there.

— Casey Stengel[1]

I can make a living telling the truth.

— Casey Stengel[2]

They say he spoke the way James Joyce wrote. So imagine *Ulysses* with a baseball twist, read aloud in clubhouses, dugouts, dining cars, hotel taverns, taxi cabs, subways.

Casey Stengel was known to talk anywhere, to anyone, about anything. When he managed the Brooklyn Dodgers, he had to stop taking cabs to Ebbets Field because drivers were turning around to talk to him while doing forty miles per hour.

So he switched to the subway—and often found himself chattering with baseball fans and getting carried well past the Ebbets Field stop.

Stengel would talk to skycaps at New York's Idlewild airport and miss two or three flights. It was more important to tidy up all the story fragments before going on his way.

He talked to newspapermen, kings, presidents, shoeshine boys, strangers on the street. If you had at least one ear, Casey would gab into it.

Here is a sampling from his many symposiums, lectures, colloquiums, and impromptu talks.

***

TOPIC: *His professional baseball debut, on May 10, 1910, with Kankakee, Illinois, of the Northern Association.*

They called me "Dutch" in them days. I dunno why, but they did. I remember the team like it was yesterday.

The league only lasted until July 4, and no records were kept. I never did find out what I was hitting. After the last game, the owners split up all the dough they pulled in and beat it.

I didn't know during the last two weeks, but I was playing for nothing. I never did collect that pay.[3]

A feller would hit me fungoes, and I'd throw the ball back in and make a hook slide in the outfield. There was an insane asylum just beyond the outfield, and they'd watch us. One guy, watching me slide in the outfield, said I'd never be back next year. "He'll be in there," said the guy, pointing at the asylum.[4]

The loonies thought I was one of theirs got loose, and the manager was inclined to agree. They didn't know I was doing three things at once, playing the outfield, getting my legs in shape, and practicing sliding.[5]

TOPIC: *A kid pitcher.*

It was early in 1914, and McGraw and Robbie owned a bar in Baltimore. Now there was no Sunday ball in Baltimore, but you could play on a racetrack outside the city.

So Robbie brought us down there to play an exhibition against the Orioles of the International League. And he wanted to do good, I guess, on account of the bar.

A young kid is pitching for the minor-league club. And you know, in those days, folks was beginning to part their hair on the left. But this kid, you could see, had sort of dark curly hair and parted it in the middle.

Well, I'm playin' right field and this kid comes to bat. And I don't play very deep because this kid after all is a pitcher on a minor-league team and probably they're saving their better pitchers for their regular games against Jersey City or someplace.

Anyway, the kid hits a ball way over my head. And this is a racetrack, mind you, and there is no fence, and I have to run like the blazes—and on a Sunday—to run this ball down. And I hold the kid to a triple.

When I get back to the bench, Robbie is a little sore and he says, "How come you let a kid hit the ball over your head like that?"

I said, "Where do you expect me to play for a bush pitcher?"

Next time the kid came up I says to Hy Myers (Brooklyn's center fielder), "I wonder how Robbie will like this?" So I'm sorta trying to show Robbie up, and I go out about thirty-five feet deeper than any right fielder has any business playing.

So do you know what happens? The kid hits the ball over my head again. And I'm runnin' and runnin'—remember this place has no fence—and I'm saying, "This is a heckuva way to spend a Sunday."

Well, the season passes and the next year the Dodgers win the pennant and we play the Red Sox in the World Series. And they play the games up there in Braves Field—instead of Fenway Park—because it can hold more people. And if you look in the record books, I think you will find that there was more people there than had ever seen a Series game before that. There was more than forty thousand.

Who's pitching for the Red Sox but that kid from Baltimore—the one who hit the two balls over my head, with his hair parted in the middle.

Hy Myers hits a home run in the first inning and they tied it—Sherry Smith was pitching for us—in the third. And the kid with the black hair shuts us out for thirteen straight innings. And they win in fourteen.

The kid goes on and, including the 1918 World Series—which is the Red Sox against the Cubs—he sets a record for shutout innings in a World Series that lasts until Whitey Ford broke it a few years ago.

In Brooklyn, there are two comics named Van and Schenck, and in their day they were pretty famous. And they were all for anything Brooklyn, and always against the Giants.

It gets to 1923 and I am in the World Series with the Giants, a team Van and Schenck don't like at all. But they like me a bit, because I used to be a Dodger. I hit a home run in the first game, and they book me for three weeks in vaudeville after the Series, though I don't know what I could do in vaudeville, except perhaps frighten people.

The Yanks win the next game and tie it up. But in the third game I hit another homer which wins the game, one to nothing, and now Van and Schenck go wild and book me all the way to Omaha.

But then that kid with the black hair from Baltimore—which the Red Sox by now have sold to the Yankees—starts hittin' the ball. And for the rest of the Series, he belts the ball all over the place, and the Yanks win the Series.

By this time Van and Schenck have forgotten me, and so has everybody else. And I don't get booked nowhere, not even to West New York. New Jersey.

But that kid with the black hair from Baltimore, and who later lives in Sudbury, Massachusetts, he goes on and does pretty good. And I'll never forget his making me chase those long balls on a racetrack with no fence in Baltimore on a Sunday.

His name? Oh, yes. It was Babe Ruth.

⊷◈⊶

TOPIC: *His studies at the Western Dental College in Kansas City.*

I'll never forget the dissecting class at the dental school. The work was naturally very serious, but once in a while fellows would fool around with those bodies when nobody was looking, and the first thing you knew, you'd find an extra thumb in your pocket.[7]

⊷◈⊶

TOPIC: *The day he got four hits as a Dodgers rookie, playing for manager Bill Dahlen in 1912.*

The last time up the bunt sign was on, and I bunted foul on the first pitch. The sign was still on when Hendrix pitched again, and with the third baseman charging, I slapped the ball past him into left field for a single. When I got back to the bench, Dahlen glared at me but didn't say anything. I guess I looked young and innocent.[8]

TOPIC: *His wife, Edna Lawson Stengel.*

The only woman which has been in my life. She has been splendid.[9]

TOPIC: *Playing for manager Wild Bill Donovan on the lowly Philadelphia Phillies.*

It got so bad just before I left that I couldn't stand dressing next to Donovan. Every time we lost a game he took it so hard you'd think we had never lost one before, although we finished last in 1920 and were a cinch to finish last again. He carried on so bad I had my locker moved to an alcove off the dressing room, and this day I am in there getting dressed after the game, when I hear Bill come in and say, "Where's Stengel?"

"He's dressing in the other room," somebody says.

And Bill says, "From now on, he'll be dressing further away than that."

Oh-oh, I says to myself. *Players are coming and going every day.* Although that didn't do any good, and I figured I was bound for Toledo or some such place. Anyway, I come out in the open, and Bill says, "I have traded you and Rawlings to the Giants. You can take your time about getting there because you do not have to report until tomorrow."

"I don't know what Rawlings has in mind," I says. "But I am going to get there before the old man has a chance to change his mind."

I didn't even go back to the place where I roomed to get my clothes. I caught the 6:15 from North Philadelphia.

TOPIC: *The day he homered for the Giants in Game 3 of the 1923 World Series and taunted the Yankees bench.*

Casey surveys Yankee Stadium on the day he is introduced as new manager of the mighty Yankees for the 1949 season. Stengel had already found success in the Bronx: He hit two game-winning home runs at The Stadium in the 1923 World Series, thumbing his nose at the New York bench after the second one.

If I hadn't listened to the advice of Judge Landis, I wouldn't be here now. Landis was a great man and a fine commissioner. He saved baseball. You didn't pull any shenanigans on him. He knew every trick in the book.

Landis was tough but he was fair. I hit a home run in Yankee Stadium to win a World Series game for the Giants, 1–0, and thumbed my nose at the Yankee players as I rounded the bases.

The Judge really tied into me for that one. "I won't permit you or anyone else to make a spectacle of himself before sixty thousand people. One more stunt like that and it will cost you your World Series check." He told me he might have taken it away then and there, but he knew the Yankee players had been riding me pretty good.[11]

TOPIC: *Brooklyn Dodgers manager Uncle Wilbert Robinson.*

You never could fool Robbie about things going on among the ballplayers. He knew almost everything and suspected the rest. Like the time Ed Appleton and I got into a fight in a Chinese restaurant on Fulton Street. Ed was a big Texan and very strong. I don't remember now what the fight was about, but it started as we were leaving the place at the top of a steep flight of stairs.

Neither of us knew how to fight, but we were 'rassling and clawing each other and went tumbling down the stairs. That took all the fight out of us, and we went back to our boarding house together. The next day when we got to the ballpark, Robbie looks at Ed with a black eye and at me with a gash on my chin and he says, "What happened to you two?"

I tell him we are in a Chinese restaurant and there is a big, ugly hoodlum at the next table and he picks on me and Ed takes a belt at him and it is pretty lively for a while but we finally get the best of him.

"It's a funny thing," Robbie said, "how there's always the third feller around."[12]

TOPIC: *Hecklers.*

There was one fellow in Pittsburgh, when I was with the Pirates, that had me stopped, though. There was hardly a day at Forbes Field that he wasn't in the right-field bleachers behind me, and all through the game he would yell, "Hey, Casey! How's Big Bess?"

You know, I never could answer him because I never found out who Big Bess was.[13]

TOPIC: *The day he reported to the Dodgers in September 1912.*

It was too late to go to the park so I checked into a hotel on Forty-eighth Street. Back home they had told me to watch my belongings when I got to New York, so I hid my suitcase under the bed, locked the door of my room, and went down to the lobby and sat there facing the elevator. If someone swiped my suitcase, I was determined that I'd get him as soon as he stepped out of the cage.

About midnight, I went upstairs, fished out the suitcase, took it to bed with me, and slept until morning.[14]

TOPIC: *The Grapefruit Incident.*

One year in spring training, someone told Uncle Robbie that he couldn't catch a baseball from a low-flying airplane with a catcher's mitt, because that was Robbie's position when he was a player. Robbie took up the challenge.

Well, somebody (Note: the culprit was Stengel) got to the pilot and supplied a couple of grapefruits instead of a baseball, which the pilot dropped out of the plane. One landed right on Robbie and he was drowned from the juice because it was a Florida grapefruit and they were in season. From that time on, any mention of grapefruit to Robbie would make him wild.

Anytime I'd be on the bench and wanted to play, I'd yell "grapefruit" loud enough for him to hear. I kept it up until he couldn't stand it and he'd let me play.[15]

TOPIC: *The double-steal.*

I used to get Robbie to let me bat after Max Carey because Carey was the best base stealer in our league. And then when I'd hit behind Carey, I'd tell Max that every time he was on second and I was on first that he was to steal third.

Well, every time he did that, I went down to second and got a stolen base and they never threw Carey out at third, and I must have had twenty-five stolen bases that season even though I couldn't run.[16]

TOPIC: *Advice to minor leaguers.*

"I knew what this was like before you were born," I told them. "You like it here? Well, it ain't bad. You could be digging coal, you know. It not only ain't—pardon me, isn't—bad, it's pretty good. But it's better up there.

"Look, you're young and you must have some ability or you wouldn't have got even this far. I'm not trying to tell you to take this too serious. Just take it serious enough. And don't ever try to fool the manager. I did, but I never succeeded and I learned better.

"Like, if I ever catch you coming into the hotel at one o'clock in the morning, don't tell me that you just went out to mail a letter. I told that to John McGraw once, and he asked me if I didn't know the last collection was at 10:30 and I could have mailed the letter then and still been in my room at eleven o'clock, which was bed-check time."

Once I surprised one of my boys coming into the hotel about two o'clock in the morning. I say I caught him by surprise because he looked surprised, and I said to him, "This ball club is paying five dollars a night for your room. Don't you think it should get more for its money?"

What should I have done? Fine him? On the kind of pay I was giving him, I would have felt like a pickpocket. It was the first time, I'm sure, he had ever stayed out late like that, and I didn't ask him what had detained him. But I'm sure he never did it again, because I was up and around and the only times I ever saw him after that was at ten o'clock at night or at the ballpark.[17]

Topic: A Mud Hens pitcher.

One day when I was managing Toledo, I pitched Roy Parmalee, a real wild guy, for some scouts to watch, hoping to sell him for a hundred thousand dollars. He began walking everybody, and with the bases full, a batter hit a liner that struck Parmalee on the left hand. He shook the left hand. I rushed from the dugout. "Shake your right hand," I ordered. "It's my left hand that's hurt," he said. "Make out like it's your pitching hand," I said. "I want to get you out of here gracefully."[18]

STARTING TOPIC: *The day in 1946 when he met Billy Martin.*

We were having tryouts for some bonus boys they had sent me. They were all dressed up in uniforms we had provided for them, and there were some other kids there, but I didn't pay any attention to them. That evening, Red Adams, our trainer, says to me, "You didn't even look at the best kid on the field today."

"Which one was he?" I asked him.

"The big-nosed kid in the ragged uniform," Red says. "He plays on the semi-pro club I manage on Sundays. Can I bring him back tomorrow?"

I tell him he can, and this time I look at the kid and I like him so much I sign him and send him to our Idaho Falls club. He does so good that I bring him back the next spring, and this time, when I tell him I'm going to send him to our club in Phoenix, he says that I'm making a mistake because he is as good as any infielder we have in the Coast League, and maybe he is right because all he does that year is to lead the Arizona State League in every-thing, such as hitting and fielding.

At the end of the season they give a big party for him and I fly in for it, and they give him a big plaque, too. And on the way home he shows it to me, and it says he hit .392, which I think is pretty good myself, but he says whoever put that on the plaque is a big jerk because he really hit .394, and I like him for the way he says it.

I bring him up to the Yankees with me and I get a big kick out of him, even if the owners do not always do so. To begin with, he is mad at me because I don't play him at second base when I have Coleman there and he is the best second baseman in the league. One day Coleman isn't feeling so good and I put Martin at second, and when he sees I have him hitting eighth, he says to me, "I suppose tomorrow I will be hitting behind the groundkeeper."

And I says, "If Coleman is feeling better tomorrow, you will be sitting right next to me on the bench, as you are right now."

You know, he wouldn't speak to me again for a week. I felt bad about that. He was the one who told me how to run the ball club.[19]

※

TOPIC: *Pittsburgh Pirates Hall of Fame third baseman Pie Traynor.*

I saw Pie come into the league with the Pirates in 1920, a big, rangy kid with a strong arm. They tried him at shortstop first, and then they moved him to third base and he was, I would have to say, the best third baseman I ever saw. So one day much later on, I asked him, "How did you become as good as you were?"

And he says, "Casey, I never believed I had made good."

You know, I never heard anybody say it that way before, but come to think of it, that was the way I operated. I figured that no matter what I had done, it wasn't good enough and I had to do better.

I tell my players, "The great ballplayers like Traynor, which he was, got to be great because they took nothing for granted about themselves but always figured they hadn't quite made it. No matter what they read about themselves in the papers, about how good they were, they weren't satisfied. So when you are on a hot streak, don't think you got it made.

"Don't get swell-headed," I tell them. "And don't get dreamy on the field. You got to be out there for a few hours, and if you don't keep your mind on the game, any minute can be a bad one for you and for the ball club." [20]

TOPIC: Managers.

The best manager I ever played for was John McGraw. Some players hated him, but they were always proud of the fact that they played for him.

Wilbert Robinson was a good manager, although he was quite the opposite. Some players criticized him. I remember five players in particular who didn't like him. All five were dumb players. I remember checking up on those five after they quit baseball, and I found out that all five were doing nothing.

Uncle Robbie was great with pitchers. He would take fellows discarded by other clubs and make winning pitchers of them again. Prime examples were Dazzy Vance, Bill Doak, Rube Marquard, Jack Combs, Jess Petty, Larry Cheney.

Speaking of Cheney reminds me that he used to pitch without a windup. He had a bum right knee and he couldn't put any pressure on it, so he had to throw without a windup. [21]

TOPIC: Don Larsen's no-windup delivery.

Well, it's a good thing for him. It's now been proven that it's all right. But up to that time he had done fairly good. He just started that two weeks ago, or three, and then in Boston two or three of our boys have started it again. And it can help some men. There's no question about it.

I remember a man that started doing it. A colored player. His name was Rogan. He played with, I believe it was the Kansas City Monarchs. And he used to pitch a lot like that, and so did Thurston after he'd won twenty games in Chicago one year, and later on when his arm didn't feel so good or anything, he found out you could throw a ball better without a windup. Possibly better.[22]

TOPIC: *Advice for a rookie reporter on his first road trip with the Yankees in the early 1950s.*

You the new man with the *Journal-American*? I'm Casey Stengel. I am the manager of the New York Yankees. You ever been to Chicago? You ever travel with ballplayers? You drink?

Lemme give you a tip. On the road, do all your drinking at the hotel bar. Don't go wandering around here and there looking for new places to drink. I'll tell you why.

Now you're sitting at the bar somewhere where people don't know you. You slip and fall off the stool. The next thing you know, some stranger's cleaned out your pockets and you're dead broke the next morning and with a hangover, too.

Now you're drinking in a hotel bar where the club stays, and you fall off the stool there. The bartender leans over and sees who it is on the floor. "Hey," he says. "This is one of them famous writers from New York. Take the key out of his pocket and help him to his room."

You get lots of trouble if more than four players go out to have a drink after a game. Player number one buys a round, player number two buys a round, and so on to player number four. If you get more than five—say, six, seven or eight, or more—they each got to buy a round, and by the time that happens, you might have somebody trying to do a tap dance on the bar or maybe pick a fight with the waiter.

You work for the *Journal-American*, right? You gotta get quotes. You write for an afternoon paper. In the morning, the people on the subway going to work back there in New York, why they're reading them morning papers. *The Times*, the *Herald Tribune*, and the rest of them. They're reading how Whitey Ford went nine and how Yogi and Mantle and Bauer and the rest of them made the runs.

Now they're on their way home from work. They want to know more than what happened. They want to read quotes from Stengel, the ballplayers. Stuff the morning writers can't fit in. Oh, if you need a quote from Stengel and I'm not there, go right ahead, but don't make me sound like I went to Harvard.[23]

TOPIC: *Baseball's Hall of Fame.*

When I was playing and winning pennants as a manager, I wasn't thinking of the Hall of Fame. Some men don't care too much about it or couldn't tell you about it because they've passed away.

Take DiMaggio and Mantle and you think of what one would do that the other couldn't do, and think of Mays and all the years I watched him. Mantle was the best distance hitter I ever saw, right or left.[24]

TOPIC: *Jackie Robinson's assertion in 1952 that the Yankees organization was anti-black:*

Casey (left) with Joe DiMaggio (center) and Mickey Mantle. Stengel managed the great DiMaggio as he ended his storied career, and the great Mantle as he began his.

I don't care who you are in this organization, you're going to get along and make the big team if you've got the ability.

We've got good coaches, a good front office, good scouts, and good minor-league managers, and we're not going to play a sap at second base just because somebody said we ought to put him there.[25]

TOPIC: *Possibly moving Mickey Mantle to shortstop in 1954:*

Everybody says I juggle the players around too much. I juggle them trying to win games, not because I like to. If I could field a regular team every day which could win every day, I'd do it.[26]

TOPIC: *His professional reputation in 1959.*

They used to call me a clown. Now I'm a genius because I win nine pennants in ten years with the Yankees. I ain't neither.

When I took the job, they said, "How could you get to manage the Yankees after all those second-division finishes in the National League? Why, the Dodgers even paid you not to manage."

They just never bothered to check into the clubs I had. They didn't bother to check my early years in the minors. I didn't have a real good club in the minors until 1944, when I managed Milwaukee to the American Association pennant, but I only had one second-division team.[27]

TOPIC: *The 1962 Mets.*

Ya know, when I beat the Cards a couple of times during the spring, I thought I had some sort of pitching staff. I learned one thing: I'll never go by what I see in spring training again.

Another thing: I'm not listening to players anymore when they tell me they can make it up here. No siree, they can't fool me anymore when they tell me their old club didn't like them, that they didn't like living in the other city and all that stuff.

Even I was not too excited about this team sometime.[28]

TOPIC: *The 1963 Mets.*

Well, it's like this. When we lose in the afternoon, I don't feel good that night. When we lose at night, I don't feel good in the morning, even after I've had breakfast. Maybe I just don't like to lose.[29]

—————◆—————

TOPIC: *His routine after home games in 1964.*

I like to walk a few blocks towards the World's Fair and hail a cab. I pull my hat down over my face, and after we drive a while I say, "Gosh, I wasted my time looking at the Fair. I shoulda gone on to Shea Stadium when I saw the lights on there, which meant they had a ball game. By the way, how did they make out?"

I found out that there's one thing the cab drivers know and that's the score of the Mets games and all about them. They give me a play-by-play all the way to New York. They listen to our games on the radio. I take Edna and we go to some steakhouse in New York and then get another cab for the hotel, and I ask about the Mets and I get it all over again. When we win, they're nice listening to.[30]

—————◆—————

TOPIC: *Attitudes of young players in 1965.*

The Youth of America. You say, "Here is the opportunity," and the Youth of America says, "How much are you going to pay me?"

It's like going to the university. They want the biggest, the best, the most. All of them twisting around. If necessary, we'll pay the bonuses, but they should earn it.

All right, go make the mistake! But quit making eight or nine of them!

They're young enough to field the ball. Are they smart enough to make the play? They protect you in the field with the appliances. They give them appliances that are like a net. The first basemen used to carry a postage stamp, now they carry fishing nets. They used to say, "Two hands for the beginners," but it counts just as much if he catches it with one hand, don't it?

They can protect you in the field, but they can't protect you with the bat. These old pitchers are too smart for them, and they're going to *stay* too smart.

The Youth of America. You bring them in and they swing as hard as they can, and you tell them to just meet the ball and they look at you. They don't know their hitting area, so they swing at balls they can't hit, and when you try to protect them, they say, "The fellow isn't playing me." If they put in the time instead of saying, "I didn't get a chance," they can make this team.[31]

TOPIC: *Looking back on his eighty-fifth birthday, would he choose a baseball career all over again?*

Baseball? Baseball? Oh, no, I wouldn't go into baseball again. I would, ah, oh, what do you call it? What's this here stuff when you get to the moon? I'd be an astronaut. I love the moon.[32]

TOPIC: *Highly paid ballplayers.*

I was glad I wasn't in them big salaries. They used to pay

off in silver and gold. How in hell could I carry all that gold around? If I had had a hundred twenty thousand dollars in silver in one pocket and a hundred thousand dollars in gold in the other, I wouldn't be living now.[33]

TOPIC: the Youth of America in 1970.

The real problem is that you don't see five people in trouble today, you see five hundred, and you won't have baseball or anything else if they commence breaking up ball games or other things.

Let me ask you why we can't communicate with those young people and I'll tell you: because there's too much fast transportation today if they want to go away from home. The only place you can get anybody to go is in an automobile.

You used to be known in your neighborhood and you had a reputation and you had the five-cent fare, too. Now they want to go someplace where they can get into trouble, and they've even got automobiles to get there. So they can go forty miles and disturb people in some other city if they don't want to be seen in their hometown. They can even go three hundred or a thousand miles away and sleep on the road besides. The reason is fast transportation, and they've all got automobiles, and there's the airplane, too. There're more places to go and you can't keep them in anymore and how can you communicate with them three hundred miles away?

If you could find something for them to do, they might stay home and listen. They might even play ball where they could earn twelve or fifteen dollars a day in spring training and get by on it, and then you could earn a swell salary and get yourself an education. Even if he came from Asia, he'd have a chance if he could play in the big leagues, and with the training complexes down south now, they promote the closeness of the races, too.

I mean we should commence to find something for them to do, and why do people go to the ballparks anyway? It must be they're better today.

It has nothing to do with long hair. I had relations that were in Columbia University and Tufts and Yale, and this is an amazing thing, they did have a burr on their heads in the pictures we've got but not the sloppy things they have today, so who is the barber who did it? They must have had one pair of clippers instead of all this fancy equipment, and still most of them looked pretty good.

But I don't mind the hair. They can wear it any way they want to as long as they don't use fast transportation to get out of their own towns. That's the thing that disappoints me when you ask if I can communicate with them. Not the hair. I wouldn't mind how long they wore it if I could find them and talk to them, and besides they didn't have wigs in those days.[34]

Topic: *Three burglars, including a neighborhood man, who tried to break into the Stengels' Glendale home while wife Edna was home and Casey was in Florida with the Mets.*

My wife, I was still in bed, she isn't feeling too good. I thought it must have been the telephone girl, see, it was like seven o'clock or a quarter to down here, calling me up to get out on the field.

We look pretty good down here, although maybe I got a problem or two. We ought to be better than them Angels. I'm still in bed, so she says some guys jiggled our back door. And in a big hurry, not thinking about her bad back, she turns on a light and nobody can see and she calls the cops.

Some neighborhood kid, sure I used to play ball with them all, there on the street. Well, I'm not home very much. I didn't get too much detail on them, see, she was still nervous.

But I guess they didn't take anything, and they're put away and all that. It didn't disturb me too much, those boys, I mean. And I want to thank everybody in the neighborhood and the cops.[35]

TOPIC: *His thoughts on seeing the new Shea Stadium for the first time.*

Well, it's hard to say. I was on the outside.[36]

TOPIC: *Winning the 1956 manager of the year award.*

Well, I'd have to say on this award of the year that naturally the first thing you have to say, that is, you should be thankful it was not given by one man but by a number of men that are authorities on baseball because they followed the sport so many years and because it's a voting proposition in which the majority share.

And therefore that's why you get the selection and feel honored because you received the selection from the men

who voted you the award, which is the writers, the sportswriters.

And the second thing is you got to thank, naturally, is
your ownership for making it possible that they own the
ball club and were successful enough to have scouts pick
up enough players to make it a very good team.

And third and last, certainly you have got to thank the
ballplayers and the coaches for cooperating great enough
to win a pennant and a world championship, and naturally that makes the manager more successful, in which
no doubt success naturally gives you, although it isn't
often you get the award just because you win a pennant
or world championship.

And the fourth thing is you got to be satisfied with
yourself that you're doing a good job with the talent
entrusted to you.[37]

TOPIC: *Smart investments.*

There you gotta be careful like. I once invested about
twenty grand in a factory up in Connecticut making
shades, you know, the kind you pull up and down.
Looked great. Every house with windows has shades. But
then some smart aleck came along and boomed Venetian
blinds. Don't know whether they ever had anything like
that in Venice. But they sure put a hole in my investment.[38]

TOPIC: *The Yankees' Far East exhibition trip in 1955.*

We made a most amazing tour. In Tokyo they are trying to
play baseball over there with small fingers. I'd like to see

it played, but you've got to have weather at the same time or else how could you play?[39]

TOPIC: *The state of the game in 1971.*

Baseball is different today. They got a lot of kids now whose uniforms are so tight, especially the pants, that they cannot bend over to pick up ground balls. And they don't want to bend over in television games because in that way there is no way their face can get on camera.

It's hard to imagine people like that—also pitchers who don't know what time it is. Pitchers today do not like it if the manager takes them out of the game. But if a man is throwing home run balls in a big park, for heaven's sake, what is he going to do in a small park?

When a fella is getting knocked around, you gotta get him out of there and wake those fellas up in the bullpen. 'Course, if you remove a pitcher, his mother is going to get mad, and the club owner who is paying him all that money is going to get mad.

I am glad sometimes that I have Edna and work in a bank. It is much safer than trying to duck people's relatives.[40]

5

TEACHER EVALUATIONS

It's unfair to compare Casey Stengel to other managers. He's a genius.

— Leo Durocher

When he didn't have much to work with, he wasn't that good.

— Al Lopez

Casey Stengel was perhaps the most brilliant manager in baseball history. No one can say for sure, because managing baseball teams is more art than science. And just try to get three graduate students to agree on the greatest post-modern something-or-another.

No one can doubt that from 1949 through 1960, Stengel rolled off the hottest streak in the history of major-league baseball skippery. In those twelve seasons, his mighty New York Yankees won ten American League pennants and seven world championships. If he presided over that kind of dominance today, Stengel would be doing underwear ads. Well, maybe on radio.

People who like Stengel point to those Yankees. He was masterful, innovative. He was enshrined in the Hall of Fame, and it wasn't for his .284 lifetime batting average or his sixty career home runs.

People who dislike Stengel point to the Dodgers, Braves, and Mets. He was a goofball, asleep in the dugout. And a stuffed monkey could have successfully managed the 1950s Yankees.

He was a genius.

No, he was a clown.

He was lucky.

No, he was good.

It's like reviews of past presidents. The reviews often depend on where the reviewer is coming from.

You decide. The following people already have.

JERRY COLEMAN:

He was very, very shrewd. A brilliant man. He might not have been a Phi Beta Kappa, but he knew more about baseball in his little finger than most people knew in their entire body.

The reason I thought he was great—I've kind of analyzed him a lot—here's a guy who, when he signed with the Yankees, the *Daily News* headline was, "Clown Takes Over Yanks." Because of his characterization when he managed Brooklyn. Just a funny guy. A riot in many ways. But the point of it is this: He had lousy ball clubs, and he tried to deflect that onto himself. He was last in Brooklyn, last in Boston.

With the Yankees, he had players and he was first ten out of twelve years. In '49, he outmanaged (Joe)

McCarthy. A couple of times we didn't win until the very end of the season. We didn't walk to the pennant every year. He was truly brilliant.

I also heard him say many times, "Well, I blew that one. That was my game. I blew that." And he'd walk into his office.

How many managers ever said that in their life? He said that several times.

ROD DEDEAUX:

I signed with him out of college, with the Brooklyn Dodgers in 1935. I've said over and over that he was the best brain I've ever known in baseball.

I remember when there was an opening for a manager with the Hollywood Stars, I told them that the ideal manager for them was Casey Stengel. He had drama about him and a lot of the theatrics. I know one of the owners thought it was a great idea, but he wasn't quite able to sell it. So Casey went to Oakland.

BOBBY BROWN:

A clown? Before he came to the club, there was that perception. But not by the people that knew him.

George Weiss, he went back years with Casey. They were associated in the Eastern League back in the '20s. I think that the two main Yankee scouts out on the coast knew him and knew that he had a profound sense of how the game should be played. I think that was probably what prompted George Weiss to hire him.

The other stuff was kind of a coverup of the vast amount of baseball knowledge that he possessed.

We weren't always favored to win the pennant. Statistics-wise that was true, but I think what people forgot is that we had guys who could play well in big games. Their skills didn't deteriorate in big games; they became enhanced. I think that's what used to carry us in a few. We had three or four guys who were superstars—that helped as well—but basically we had guys who could play well in tight situations.

DARIO LODIGIANI:

I played for him in '47 and '48 in Oakland. He was a good manager out here. They called us the Nine Old Men. They hadn't won a pennant in twenty-seven years, I think.

I was fortunate enough to have played for a lot of great managers. Connie Mack and Jimmy Dykes and Lefty O'Doul. Casey was a good manager.

I'll say one thing about Casey Stengel, and I saw it when he went to the Yankees: He was the best manager I ever played for in handling pitchers. He had the knack of getting the pitcher out of there before he got in trouble.

EDDIE JOOST, who played under Stengel on the 1943 Braves and managed the Philadelphia Athletics against Stengel's Yankees in 1954:

With the Braves, it was a disaster, including myself. A complete disaster. I could never consider the fact that he was a great manager. He was never a good manager—you could look up the record. The only successful job he had was with the Yankees.

I don't think he was really consistent about knowing talent. He just went along and did things the way the old-timers did. They play a set number of people, pitch a set number of people.

Basically, what I saw of Casey is that he was just not involved in being the manager in his job there in Boston. He was just another individual who came out to the ballpark and tried to steer a bunch of people into playing baseball.

I don't think he was a baseball genius, which he was termed to be when he was with the Yankees. The talent he had in Boston was not comparable to the two teams, as I call it, that he had with the Yankees. They were good enough for two teams.

Managing is something, in my opinion, where you try to keep people involved in what they're doing and happy about it—not get agitated or aggravated about your job out there. Stengel was good at that with the Yankees, but he wasn't good at that with any other team.

He didn't have the talent. But if he were a genius, the teams that he had would have at least improved. But none of them did.

He became a genius because he had a team that was really two teams in New York, and each of them could have beaten any other team in the American League at that time.

When I was managing the Athletics, we had decent players, nothing that would say we were going to win the pennant or finish in the first division. But each time you went to make a move against the Yankees, they would just laugh at you. They'd just bring in so-and-so to hit, or another guy to pitch.

I just said to myself, *There's just no way you could beat this guy. Each time he makes a change, he brings a guy in who's just as good or better.* That's the way it was.

He wasn't a great manager. He was a manager like the rest of us.

BOBBY RICHARDSON:

I think he was good because, number one, you were kept loose on the ball club; number two, he was great with the press; number three, he surrounded himself with great coaching.

And with the talent he had, he was perhaps ideal at that time for our ball club.

I think his strong point was dealing with the press. He enjoyed that. And he had the best guys in the world for actually running the ball club. Frankie Crosetti actually ran the ball club. Jim Turner ran the pitchers. Casey didn't have a lot to do during the games.

I think it's been documented that he was known to fall asleep during games. I was playing, but I've heard my teammates say that he would wake up and look around. I don't think I saw it that much because we had Crosetti and Jim Turner. We looked to those guys. The lineup was made out. Crosetti gave the signals. Whether they came from Stengel or not, I don't know.

TOMMY BYRNE:

He got along great with Jim Turner and his other coaches. Turner was oriented to the National League. I guess he

PHOTO COURTESY OF JOSEPH CARLISTO

Casey kicks back and raises a finger to make a point. He was always willing to talk to anybody, anywhere, about anything, but sometimes his players were not willing to listen.

was around when old Casey was in that league. They had a good rapport. And of course Dickey got along with him. Crosetti, of course, he coached third base all the time Casey was there.

The Crow was the brains. He could keep up with things better than anyone else.

HANK BAUER, *Stengel's onetime Yankee who went on to manage the Kansas City Athletics, the Baltimore Orioles, and the Oakland Athletics:*

I'll also say this: He had the horses. I managed and I know one thing: Ballplayers make managers. Managers don't make ballplayers.

I think the big secret in managing, like Casey did, is to have a good pitching coach. Don't mess up your pitching staff or your rotation. Jim Turner was a great pitching coach, Frank Crosetti was a great guy at third, and Bill Dickey was a great guy at first. So Casey couldn't do much wrong.

AL LOPEZ, *whose 1954 Cleveland Indians and '59 Chicago White Sox beat Stengel's Yankees for American League pennants:*

He helped the Yankees. He came in at an opportune time, when the other guys were getting older—DiMaggio and Rizzuto.

He was real good with kids. I think that helped with Mantle and Gil McDougald, Whitey Ford.

He liked to change guys around, liked to put them in different positions. I didn't manage like that.

I chased him for eight or ten years. I finally beat him twice. They were hard to beat.

EDDIE JOOST:

Jim Turner was the pitching coach. He was the one who ran that pitching staff; he knew what the hell was going on. Crosetti was the third-base coach. The point is, Stengel didn't run that ball club.

Casey didn't give the signs at third base; Crow gave the signs. And Turner was the guy who ran the bullpen. Anybody will tell you that.

Casey was loved by the sportswriters because he would sit down and talk to them on the bench. There would be twenty or thirty of them. He'd give them the

Stengelese stuff, and they were eating it up. This was when he was managing the Yankees.

I believe that Turner and Crosetti ran that ball club. Stengel, of course, was the glamour boy over there.

RON HUNT:

I respected him. I respected him for what he was. He was an individual that had a job to do. He did it well. And he surrounded himself with good coaches that could handle the offense, defense, pitching, whatever.

Basically, Casey took care of the press. But don't mistake and think that he wasn't the boss. The coaches just had their jobs. Casey was the boss.

RON SWOBODA:

You have to know that Casey with the Mets completely understood what his role was—to entertain the media, and keep them from turning on the franchise. The team wasn't going to win anything. There was no way, no chance.

And he understood that expansion back then was a blueprint for a lousy team. In those days, you couldn't augment expansion with free agency, so you were going to be horseshit. And the Mets were.

I really felt like his legend was diminished by his experience with the Mets. He had all those championship teams with the Yankees. I think because the Mets were such a laughingstock, and that he played into that, that it did in some ways diminish his legend.

In a way, that should not have happened. To some people, that's all they remember about Casey Stengel. They forget the guy that handled those great Yankee teams and won championships.

At least it was great that he was still alive when we won a World Series. That was one of the greatest parts about it. He was there a lot in '69. It was just so gratifying to know that Stengel saw that.

ROD KANEHL:

Casey Stengel is the only man who could have managed those 1962, '63, '64 Mets teams in New York. We came back to New York with a good ball club but no pitching. We didn't draw two million that first year, but the fans loved us. He filled the writers' columns with whatever it took, and the writers were happy with that.

And he led the parade up Broadway. I can't think of any other manager who could have done that.

I just think he was the ideal person to create this "Let's Go Mets" stuff, this underdog business. We didn't let him down. We were underdogs.

A strength: Stengel could read players. He was famous for playing hunches that worked. The less charitable say it was because he was playing hunches with the 1950s Yankees—loaded dice. Others say he had the magic touch. He had the credentials for great gut instincts—guts and tons of experience. There were all those years of watching all those baseball games. For Stengel, it was like listening to the same album a hundred times: He knew which song was coming next. **COLEMAN:**

He knew you better than you knew yourself. In a week, he had you down cold.

<hr>

MARK FREEMAN:

He had a knack. He would sleep during the games. Crosetti or somebody would say, "Casey, we need a pinch-hitter."

He'd wake up and he'd say, "Carey. Go hit."

Sure enough, Andy Carey would go up and hit a double.

<hr>

GIL MCDOUGALD, *Yankees infielder for Stengel, 1951–60, and one of Casey's favorites:*

Casey always knew when a man was ready to pinch-hit or not. And I could read him like a book. He'd come by on the bench and stand and look you right in the eye. Like he'd stop in front of Bobby Brown, and he'd say something like, "Bauer," or "Woodling, grab a bat." Still looking at Brown. Casey was a hunch manager. No statistics for him. He'd look at a guy and get the feeling. It was funny.[1]

<hr>

RALPH HOUK:

My locker was close to his when I was a coach in The Stadium. I could sometimes hear what was going on with him in the press conference after the game. He had a way of handling the press that was unique.

Like one time, he put the wrong pinch-hitter up. I think it was (Elston) Howard. It was a right-hand pitcher and he sent Ellie up to pinch-hit. Casey tried to call him back in, but it was too late; he had been announced. It turned out, believe it or not, that Ellie hit a home run into the left-field bleachers.

Afterward, the press said, "Geez, Casey, we looked it up and Ellie never really hit that guy."

Casey said, "Yeah, but you don't realize how many line drives he's hit off of him."

So he always had an answer. He always said, "Remember when you're talking to the press, they don't know what you know about your players."

Criticism: Sometimes he looked into a player's eyes and missed—by a mile. **Art Johnson,** *who pitched for Stengel's Boston Braves:*

One day I was going to start, I was sitting on the bench with Casey. This young, skinny kid came in to pitch batting practice. He had just been signed out of Buffalo, New York, and was eventually going to be sent to the minor leagues. This was in 1941.

He went out and he pitched about twenty minutes. He had this perfect delivery. Every ball was a strike. After about twenty minutes, Casey said to me, "What do you think?"

I said, "I don't know. He's kinda skinny. He doesn't weigh but 150, 155 pounds. He doesn't seem to be throwing with much speed. I just don't think he's a good prospect. I don't think he'll ever make it."

Casey agreed with me.

But he made it—it was Warren Spahn.

※

In 1935, Brooklyn high school kid **PHIL RIZZUTO**, *who grew up to be a Hall of Fame shortstop with the Yankees, had a tryout with Stengel's Dodgers. Rizzuto, who played for Casey, 1949–56:*

He told me, "You're too small. Go get yourself a shoebox. It's the only way you're going to make a living."

I never let him forget it. We never quite got along, Casey and me. I never got mad, never held a grudge, but that stayed with me. Made me work harder. By '49, I didn't need a shoebox anyway. The kid in the clubhouse polished my spikes for me.[2]

※

Criticism: By the time he hit age seventy, Casey wasn't sharp anymore. Evidence was his bizarre decision in the 1960 World Series to start ace Whitey Ford in Games 3 and 6 instead of Games 1, 4, and 7. New York lost to the Pirates in Game 7, 10–9. **BOBBY RICHARDSON**:

I don't want to be critical, but when you have Whitey Ford—who was the best pitcher in baseball—and you don't start him in the first game of the '60 World Series, somebody is not making the right decisions. I think that's probably why they made the decision to go ahead and make a change.

His comment was, "We'll wait until we get to the big ballpark." But with Whitey, it didn't matter what ballpark he was in.

I think a lot of us thought maybe (Casey) knew something we didn't know. Some of us went to Whitey and said, "What's wrong with you?" He said, "Nothing." We were just wondering how you could not start him.

BOB CASE:

The biggest regret in his career—he told me until the day he died—was that he should have brought in Ford in relief in the seventh game in 1960, instead of Ralph Terry.

Criticism: The Yankees responded slowly to the integration of black players into major-league baseball, and that was fine with Stengel. Some have gone as far as to call him racist. **ROY CAMPANELLA JR.,** *son of the black Hall of Fame catcher for the Brooklyn Dodgers:*

Sitting so close, I could also hear the racist remarks coming from the opposing dugout that were directed at my father, Jackie Robinson, and the other black Dodgers. Eddie Stanky, when he managed the Cardinals, was particularly abusive and encouraged his players to emulate him. Casey Stengel is so beloved that it may surprise some people that he was particularly insulting to blacks; he was a racist who used the word "nigger" as if he thought it were appropriate.[3]

AL JACKSON, *black pitcher for Stengel's New York Mets:*

I never saw any evidence at all of anything like that. I would tell you if I did. I didn't.

———❖———

Stengel and Jackie Robinson conducted a lifelong, bitter feud. **ROBERT W. CREAMER,** *Stengel biographer:*

For all of this, it is doubtful that Stengel was a bigot. His distaste for Robinson—or *Robi'son*, as he always pronounced it—may have been racial at heart (if not overt, then at least latent), but in retrospect it seems to have been caused more by professional jealousy. Robinson was awfully good, precisely the talented all-around player that Stengel admired and would love to have on his own team. The fact that Robinson was not on his team, that he was the enemy—and an irritating, overbearing enemy— goaded him. . . .

Casey was . . . a racist only in the casual, unthinking way most of his generation of Americans were. Racial and ethnic slurs were characteristic of his era . . . and his own sarcastic, parodying nature jumped on a man's obvious features: floppy ears, big nose, black skin. But when he played against the black army team at Fort Huachuca, Arizona, during his barnstorming tour in the winter of 1919–20, he admired the skills of the outstanding black players so much that he recommended them to James Wilkinson, who was putting together the Kansas City Monarchs. (Historian) John Holway says that black players gave Stengel credit for creating the Monarchs.[4]

———❖———

MAURY ALLEN, *Stengel biographer who covered Casey's Mets for the* New York Post:

The first black to play for the Yankees was Elston Howard, in 1955. In one game, there's a hit-and-run play, and Elston Howard is on first base with a single. John Blanchard was the batter, a left-handed hitter. He hit a ground ball to the right side, and the second baseman fielded the ball and he threw to second and he got Elston Howard out at second. Pretty difficult to do on a hit-and-run play.

After the game, Casey says, "When I finally get a nigger, I get the only one who can't run."

Well, everyone who heard it was kind of taken aback a little.

The general perception was that he was not terribly comfortable around Elston Howard and around black people. But as time went on and he realized what a good player Elston Howard was, they became very close. He loved Elston Howard.

He really changed. I think the bottom line to Casey's judgment of any ballplayer was, if the player played hard, to the best of his ability, Casey liked him.

Now, he had a thing with Jackie Robinson, an ongoing thing. And it really didn't have to do with race. It had to do with Jackie Robinson's abrasive style of play. Stealing bases when Casey thought you didn't do that. Taking the extra base. Tormenting the pitcher when he was on third. Plus, Jackie Robinson, in the vernacular, had a big mouth. And he yelled at Casey. This was an ongoing thing. It stayed throughout Casey's life.

Robinson was very critical of him. I had written a column in 1963. A couple of players on the Mets had said that Casey is losing it, he's seventy-three years old, he's falling asleep on the bench. So I interviewed a bunch of the players, and a lot of them said no, he was alert, he wasn't falling asleep. Once in a while his head is down, but he always knows what's going on.

Jackie Robinson gave an interview to Howard Cosell about the fact that Casey is losing it, he should retire. So I wrote what I considered a stinging column about Jackie Robinson—who happened to be my hero. But Jackie attacked Casey Stengel, and I thought it was very unfair and it really related to Jackie's animosity toward Casey going back to from '49 on.

Jackie Robinson called me up the next day. He said, "That was a real nasty column you wrote. You were very sarcastic and angry." I said, "Jackie, I thought what you said and the way you attacked Casey was not very fair." It was an ongoing disagreement we had.

My general sense of Casey Stengel, from Jackie Robinson's time on, is that he was not a racist. You have to recognize that he was born in 1890. There weren't too many white people who were born in 1890 who were terribly comfortable with black people. That's just the way the world was.

ROD KANEHL:

What made Robinson so mad is when Casey brought in (Bob) Kuzava to pitch to him in that World Series. Kuzava was a left-hander, and he brought him in to face Robinson. That's when he hit that popup that Billy Martin caught. Robinson always felt that Casey was showing him up by bringing in a left-hander. Casey told me this: that he really got that guy and he loved it.

I think Casey was a little prejudiced. I remember being on the bench in Philadelphia and Wes Covington

PHOTO FROM THE AUTHOR'S COLLECTION

Casey shows off souvenirs from the Yankees' Far East tour after the 1955 season. At age sixty-five, he was still willing to do practically anything for a good laugh.

was at the plate. Casey was saying, "Get that load of coal out of there." He called him a load of coal.

Casey might have been a little prejudiced, but if you could play, it didn't matter to him what color you were.

BOB CASE:

I was around this guy every day for ten years. I couldn't say a negative thing about him. Like some of these people try to say that he was prejudiced. That's a crock of shit. Casey was born in 1890 in Kansas City. When he was twenty years old, it was 1910. The whole world was prejudiced in those days.

ELSTON HOWARD, who played for Stengel's Yankees, 1955–60:

I can't say enough about him because of what he did for me. I was the first black player the Yankees signed, and he made breaching the color line easier for me.

He told hotel managers he would not allow the team to stay if I wasn't welcome, too.[5]

Criticism, led by then-radio reporter Howard Cosell:
By the time he managed the Mets, Stengel was out
of it, snoozing on the bench, and should be packed
off to California and retirement. **BOB SALES,** *who*
covered the Mets and Stengel for the New York
Herald Tribune:

The players said he slept in the dugout. He probably
couldn't stand watching them play.

On the other hand, Cosell was very smart. Cosell saw
that everybody was being very nice to Casey. Cosell went
the other way on his radio show, started hammering him.
Said he was old, he was senile, he was sleeping in the
dugout. He had some of the players—Warren Spahn was
one of them—whining to him. Cosell did postgame radio
shows for the Mets, and he blasted Casey all the time.
That was actually really smart, to start a feud with the
biggest guy. That helped make Cosell's reputation.

ROD KANEHL:

He'd doze off. He knew exactly what was going on. He
wouldn't miss anything, but he would doze a bit. Warm
afternoons. Afternoon games. When it's three o'clock and
you're seventy years old, eighty years old, you need to
take a nap.

I'd rattle the bats to let him know that something was
coming up that he ought to be aware of. If there was a
change that needed to be made, I'd make some noise.

We had a catcher named Jesse Gonder. He and I would
run around together a little bit in New York. He would

take me up to Harlem, and I would take him to places in Midtown. I would rattle a bat or something when there was a pinch-hit situation or there was a situation where I might get a chance to go in. I was always ready, looking for an opportunity to play.

Jesse called me over to the edge of the bench one time. He said, "Rod, if you don't play, they'll never find out."

In '63, he called a meeting late in the season in L.A. That's when the talk came out that Casey was sleeping on the bench. Jackie Robinson was getting on him. He called this meeting about sleeping on the bench.

He went around to all the players and he said, "And I want to mention one other thing. If you guys were as old as I am, and have to stay up as late as I do checking you guys in at night, you'd sleep on the bench, too. But I'm not going to tell the writers that."

<hr>

Ron Swoboda:

He did sleep in the dugout, and sometimes players would screw with him. Ballplayers could be cruel that way.

<hr>

Galen Cisco:

I'm not saying he didn't doze off once in a while. But he knew what was going on.

We were playing the Dodgers up at Vero Beach in spring training. There were no dugouts there, just a bench where you sat out in front of the stands. Casey was kind of nodding a little. It was late afternoon, it was hotter than heck.

Somebody hit a double with a man on first.

Anyway, the guy who was on first was coming home and he slid. I think Kanehl was sitting next to Casey and he yelled in Casey's ear: *"Slide! Slide!"*

Casey jumped up kind of startled, and yelled, "HIT THE DECK!"

JACK LANG:

He didn't fall asleep on the bench; he slept with one eye open. He was a very, very alert man.

People said he fell asleep on the bench. He might have dozed off between innings, but when anything was going on in the game, he was as alert as you could possibly be.

There was a time in Saint Petersburg during batting practice at Huggins-Stengel Field.

Somebody said, "Casey, there's an old friend of yours behind the batting screen. He was with you when you broke in, in Kankakee."

You know, Stengel is now in his seventies. The guy goes over and he says to Casey, "You don't recognize me, do you?" The guy's probably ninety.

Casey says, "No, I don't."

The guy says, "I used to run the café on Main Street in Kankakee."

Casey says, "That's right. You used to give out meal tickets. For five dollars, we could eat our meals there for a week. And the league folded in the middle of the week and I still had two dollars left on my card."

The old guy almost fell over. Casey is telling him he still has two dollars left on his meal card, from like 1902.

Casey had that kind of memory.

Bob Case:

His memory was unbelievable. He would have been successful in no matter what he did. People thought he was a clown. This was a guy who was worth millions of dollars when he died. Millions. He was the president of like seven banks. He had stock in Coca-Cola, stock in Nash-Rambler. He lived in a beautiful, beautiful home. He was sharp.

Galen Cisco:

I'll tell you what kind of mind he had. At one time he managed the Toledo Mud Hens. One time in the lobby, I was sitting with him in the afternoon, waiting to go to the ballpark. Lobbies always had a lot of couches and chairs at that time.

We got to talking about him managing Toledo. He went through his entire lineup, position by position. Told me all about every player he had, what he could do and what he couldn't do. And what kind of year they had. It convinced me right there. His mind was still very, very good. I'm glad I had the opportunity to be around him.

Al Jackson:

Did I see signs of age? I saw signs of youth, too. He just had a motor that was running all the time. We were in awe at the way he could keep going.

People talk about him going to sleep. I was with him the whole time with the Mets. I never did see him sleep. If he did, maybe I missed it—maybe *I* was off sleeping somewhere.

———◆———

Criticism: Stengel's sarcastic wit bordered on cruelty. For a player's manager, he could appear heartless toward his players. A story from his Braves tenure: One of his players who made an out was walking absent-mindedly near the backstop when the ball rolled to his feet. He picked it up and threw to the opposing catcher, who gratefully caught it and tagged the Braves runner trying to score from third on a wild pitch. Buddy Hassett, who advanced to third on the play, asked Stengel, who was coaching at third, "Do you think they'll give him an assist?"

A moment later, the player was not paying attention in the dugout when he was struck in the head and knocked down by a foul line drive. Stengel was among those who hurried to the fallen player, but Casey was the one who said, "Don't touch him. Leave him lay there. It might drive some sense into the son of a bitch." **MAX WEST:**

That was me. The dugout in Braves Field was very close to home plate. The water fountain was right at the end of the dugout.

I got up and went over to get some water, and as I turned on the faucet and I opened my mouth, Paul Waner fouled this ball off and it hit me right in the mouth. My lips and my mouth were hamburger, so I didn't hear anything Casey said.

ED LINN, in 1965:

The most persistent criticism of Stengel is that he would rip his players apart to his friends, the newspapermen, for an item or a laugh. Clete Boyer, for one, never made any great secret of his distaste for Stengel. "You open the paper in the morning," Clete would say, "and you read how lousy you are."

You didn't always have to wait for the paper. Casey once conducted a visitor to the batting cage while Jerry Lumpe, a good all-around infielder, was spraying line drives to all fields. "That's Lumpe," Casey said loudly. "He's a great hitter until I play him."

The only good defensive catcher the Mets have ever had is Chris Cannizzaro (whom Casey always calls Canzoneri). When Cannizzaro made two errors in one game, Casey told his writers, "He's a remarkable catcher, that Canzoneri. He's the only defensive catcher in baseball who can't catch."

Everyone laughed heartily, except possibly Cannizzaro.[6]

DAVE EGAN, the caustic Boston Record columnist who made a career out of tormenting Ted Williams, knew something of nasty wit. He was the one who wrote that the Boston cabbie who hit Stengel and broke his leg in 1943 should be feted as "the man who did the most for Boston baseball in 1943." Egan also had this to say about Stengel:

He is, of course, a very funny fellow whose witticisms are

appreciated by everybody except the butt of his heavy-handed quips.[7]

———◆———

MARK FREEMAN, *pitcher on Stengel's 1959 Yankees:*

I was one of those guys who would go to spring training every year. About the time when I thought I was going to make the team, they'd get Bob Turley or Don Larsen or somebody.

One year I thought for sure that I had made the team. During one of the spring training games, Gil McDougald was playing third. He came over after I had walked somebody and he said, "Don't worry about it. Casey said you've got the team made."

About four days later, Casey called me into his office. He said, "Okay, get your bags packed. You're going north with the club."

All my life I had been waiting to hear that.

Then Casey said, "And you're getting off in Richmond."

That was the Triple-A farm club of the Yankees.

When I had to get off at Richmond, I was really mad. He was sleeping in the club car, sitting up. The train was parked there for some time, and I decided that I was going to let him have a piece of my mind. He had been jacking me around, I thought.

I went down there and I confronted him. I said, "You haven't been fair with me and you know it."

He was drunk. He said, "You goddamn college punk. You couldn't pitch for the Yankees."

I said, "You're a no-good son of a bitch."

He started screaming and I just ran. I left the car. He came out onto the platform and he was yelling down the station, calling me "wise-ass college punk."

But after that, I went back up and he was just great with me. He didn't hold a grudge. He just didn't have that in him. Truthfully, he just did not have that in him.

TOMMY BYRNE:

He wouldn't hold a grudge. I'll tell you, he had a pretty good chance to dislike me. I had a couple of pretty good years when I was there, and then they traded me away. He called me into his office there and he said, "Well, I'm going to wish you well. You did a good job for us."

Later on, when they were thinking about whether to bring me back, he was in favor of it. Casey and I hit it off pretty good. He did not hold grudges.

Maybe sometimes he did. EDDIE JOOST:

I broke my wrist and I couldn't play. We were going on the last road trip and I went up to the office. Mr. Quinn was the owner at that time. I went up to the office and I said, "Look, this is ridiculous. We're going on a twenty-one-day road trip all around the league, and I can't play. Why should I have to go? If I could play, I'd be happy to go. Why don't you just let me go home, call it a season, and I'll see you next year?"

They sat there and listened to me and said, "That's fine. We agree. You have an injury. You can't play. Go on home, we'll see you next spring."

So this was during the war, of course, and I had a hell-uva time getting home. When I did finally get home, I was there about one day and in comes this special-delivery airmail letter.

Indefinitely suspended without pay for jumping the ball club.

6

Tuesdays with Casey

He had life, man. Oh, did he have life.

— Al Jackson

He lived life, that's for sure. To the fullest.

— Max Carey

Have a beer with Casey Stengel, and you'd learn an awful lot about Zack Wheat, the relative velocity of a grapefruit dropped from an airplane, the proper way to take a lead from third base, the right-field wall at Ebbets Field, and how he and his brother Grant used to pull the potato trick back on the sandlots of Kansas City.

Have a lot of beers with Casey Stengel, or just spend quality time around him with no refreshments at all, and you would probably learn some deeper stuff.

By all accounts, Stengel knew a thing or two about life. And not just because he eked out so many years of it. He knew the ingredients for a good existence as well as he knew the ingredients for a good baseball team.

You build a baseball team around the catcher, short-stop, and center fielder. You build a life around love, passion, curiosity, dedication, friends, and humor.

It is easy to picture Stengel as an old professor. At any stage of life, former students could drop by and learn something about what to do next.

How to go through life splendidly, from Casey Stengel as told to his friends:

1. GROW UP WITHOUT GROWING OLD.

Stay lively. Stay smart. Don't get stale, stupid, stuffy, and sleepy.

RON SWOBODA:

You would see him at Old-Timers Days at Shea. You'd see him in the locker room and he'd look like he was ninety.

Then he would become that Casey Stengel character. He'd bounce up the steps like he was fifty and run out there and click his heels. He really did turn on the crowd. He really did perform in front of people.

He was a legend. That's the truth. People don't manage baseball teams when they're seventy years old. How many have? I was twenty years old when I first saw him, and he was seventy-something.

And we're wearing the same uniform.

He looked seventy years old, for Christ's sake. He drank and he lived hard. But the eyes—his eyes were an incredible, youthful blue. Inside this face that looked like it came off of Rushmore, there were these dancing blue eyes in there, man. It was amazing.

MAURY ALLEN:

In 1964, the Mets played an exhibition game at West Point. It was sort of a rainy day, and he slipped on the concrete as he was walking to the field. He sat through a whole game, and when the game was over, he went back to New York. We were all there covering the game, and we didn't know that this had happened. When we went back to his hotel, we found out that he had broken his wrist.

He had been taken to the hospital and had the wrist set. About an hour and a half later, with his wrist set and his arm in a sling, he came back and he sat in the hotel lobby and talked all about the game. How the Mets looked good, against the Army college team.

His enthusiasm was still there. His line was, "I broke my wrist. I didn't break my head."

TIM HORGAN, *longtime* Boston Herald *columnist:*

I'll never forget the World Series when they played the Dodgers. I guess it was 1955.

We stayed in the hotel right next to Grand Central Station, and we went back there after the game. We got in the lobby and there's a mob there. There must have been a hundred people.

I look in the middle and there's Casey. Right in the middle of it. And he was entertaining everybody. He was talking to the fans and laughing. I remember this was incredible. Most of these managers wouldn't smile if it broke their heart.

CHUCK STEVENS:

The first time I met Case, Vern Stephens and I were rookies with the Browns. We trained in San Antonio. Case had the Braves there; they were training there. Obviously, we played each other continually and even went down into Monterrey, Mexico, and played. I got to know him pretty good.

We had a big parade in Mexico, and we all walked in it. There were a lot of people on both sides of the street.

And old Case was walking right down the middle of the street having the time of his life. That was right in his wheelhouse. If you can imagine all the Mexican residents lining the streets, the bands and everything.

And Casey, you'd think, was the grand marshal of all grand marshals. He's prancing and he's waving. He had that funny walk, with his old bowlegs. He was really putting on the show, going to the curbs, patting everybody.

BOB CASE:

After he retired, they gave him a title of something like vice president of the Mets.

He was very busy; he wasn't just sitting around. People would honor him. He did a dog food commercial; he did quite a few commercials.

In later years, he lived for those Old-Timers Games. He loved going to those Old-Timers Games. I went with him to quite a few of them.

Casey was so funny. He was adaptable to everything.

He was a character. He never knocked hippies or anything. He was not narrow-minded. He acted like a young guy. He even he dressed flashy in those days. Wild ties. He dyed his hair—Edna did it, actually. He thought it was hilarious; he kind of did it as a joke. That was probably '67 or '68 when he dyed his hair.

<hr/>

SWOBODA:

One time during his retirement, we had one of these welcome-home dinners with the Mets. I remember him sitting all by himself. I remember walking up to him in the backstage area, and I sat down with him.

I went, "Casey, would you have had as much fun if you had gone on and become a dentist?"

His response really showed to me how intelligent this guy was, how complete his thought was. He said, "Well, I'll tell you what. If I was going to be a dentist, I'd be an orthodontist."

I said, "Why?"

He said, "Because people will buy things for their kids they won't buy for themselves."

Wisdom. You know?

<hr/>

MAURY ALLEN:

He was the most intelligent and most aware person in baseball that I met in forty-five years in the business. Remarkable. He knew about everything.

He knew politics. He would talk about elections in different states. He was an inveterate reader of newspapers.

He read every newspaper. He knew everything that was going on in the world.

⎯⎯⎯⎯⎯⎯

BOB SALES, who covered Stengel's Mets for the New York Herald Tribune:

He was a smart guy about more than baseball.

I remember being at an All-Star Game. Kennedy was the president; it had to be '62, '63. Kennedy came through the dressing room and just shook hands and did the things that all presidents do.

Casey was just musing. He said to Kennedy, "Boy, would I like to talk to you for about an hour or three about the economy."

⎯⎯⎯⎯⎯⎯

ROD KANEHL:

We were both from Missouri. One day after a game in '62, he came over to me and said, "Be over at such-and-such hotel with a coat and tie on."

They were honoring Walter Cronkite at the Missouri Society in Manhattan. Casey and I sat at the same table with Walter Cronkite.

Casey could talk with anyone. Casey doesn't miss a beat with anyone. He doesn't bore anybody.

⎯⎯⎯⎯⎯⎯

MAURY ALLEN:

We were on a flight that was delayed. We were going from Los Angeles to Houston. The Mets had played in Los

Angeles. There were some plane problems, and the plane went to Dallas. We laid over in the Dallas airport for four hours. Now it's five o'clock in the morning, and finally the plane takes off for Houston. When we get to Houston, it's now seven, seven-thirty in the morning. Everybody is really tired.

I was twenty-nine years old and Casey was seventy-three. And Casey turned to the traveling secretary in front of all of us and he says, "Tell the writers if they want to talk to me, I'm up in my room being embalmed."

A lot of us went upstairs and went to sleep and got up three o'clock in the afternoon. Later on we talked to other people. They told us that Casey was in the hotel lobby at eight o'clock in the morning, an hour after we had arrived. Obviously he didn't sleep. He went up, took a shower, and came down.

JACK LANG:

He liked to sit and have a couple of drinks. It was his way of relaxing. I never saw him drunk. I'm sure he was inebriated sometimes, but I never saw him that he couldn't handle himself.

One night we came up from Los Angeles after a night game. We flew into San Francisco. When we got there, the California Women's Republican Club was holding a convention at our hotel.

When we pulled into the lobby at about two o'clock in the morning, all these women were there, waiting to see Casey. All these fifty-, sixty-year-old women, all waiting to see Casey Stengel. He stood there talking to them for about an hour.

Finally, when he went to bed, it had to be three o'clock in the morning. Eight o'clock in the morning, he's one of the first ones out for breakfast.

He didn't require a lot of sleep.

ROD KANEHL:

I moved from Springfield to Los Angeles in '68. I would go up to Glendale and visit him. We'd sit around and talk. In '69, I was interested in getting back into the game. I went to Stengel to talk to him about it.

He said, "Let's think about this." He decided the Angels would be the best opportunity for me to get back into the game. Bob Reynolds was the owner with Gene Autry at the time.

His offices were there on Wilshire in Westwood. Casey said, "If you can get an appointment with Bob Reynolds, we'll have lunch with him and we'll talk about getting you back in the game."

So I set up an appointment. And I went and picked up Casey and we went to this lunch.

This was in August of 1969. We had a nice lunch, and all Casey could talk about is that the Mets were going to win the pennant. That's all he could talk about. He said the Mets were going to win the pennant because they could win on the road and you know they can win at home. And they were eight games behind the Cubs at the time.

When the lunch broke up, Reynolds took me aside and said, "Rod, call me next week and we'll talk about your future."

Casey had done all the talking, and it was about the Mets and how they were going to win the pennant. And of course, he was right.

Casey sits on a steamer trunk as the Yankees break camp in the spring of 1960. It would be his final season with the Yankees, who fired him after losing the World Series to Pittsburgh in seven games.

MAURY ALLEN:

After the Yankees firing, in 1960, they had a press conference at the Savoy Hotel.

It was typical Casey Stengel. He was kind of grouchy during the press conference. The Yankees tried to control the press conference by saying Casey was "retired," that he was paid a good sum of money to retire. Of course, he was fired.

So he began talking at the press conference about the fact that he was fired. "You can call it what you want, but I was fired." The more he talked, the more the writers, who had a lot of affection for him, started to laugh at the things that he said. After a while, it became kind of a rowdy, humorous press conference.

By the time it was over, he had taken over the press conference. In other words, the Yankees thought that they were holding a press conference, but because of his personality and his relationship with the media, Casey had taken over the press conference.

By the time it ended and we walked out the door together, he was in top Stengelese form. Doing his act, double-talking, his humor. That's really what he was all about, a guy that enjoyed the humorous aspect of life.

After it was all over, a couple of us continued to talk to him.

We were walking down Fifth Avenue in Manhattan. People recognized him and yelled at him, waved at him. Of course, he waved back and kidded with everybody.

We got to a traffic light at Fifth Avenue and Fifty-second Street, a busy intersection. The light changed and he just ran across the street. He was going back to his hotel; he stayed in the Essex House. He just ran across the street and waved. And that was the last time I saw him as the Yankee manager.

2. FIND TRUE LOVE, AND HOLD ONTO IT FOREVER.
Stengel married Edna Lawson in 1924, and they were crazy about each other until his death in 1975. Edna, who had been in decline for several years, died in 1978 at age eighty-three.

DARIO LODIGIANI:

Edna was a wonderful person. She was an opposite of Casey. He'd put on that Pagliacci front, like a big clown. Mrs. Stengel was as solid as a rock.

CHUCK STEVENS:

She was a nice lady. Don't forget her. I remember one time we were at a luncheon at Dodger Stadium. At the luncheon,

Edna was with Case, and I had my first grandson with me. He was kind of a little guy.

Edna came up and walked him all over that luncheon. They were that kind of people.

ART JOHNSON:

Edna was a lovely, lovely lady. They were absolutely crazy about each other. We all could tell.

She used to travel the eastern circuit—New York, Philadelphia. They were inseparable when we traveled and she was along. You'd see them in the dining room, and they'd be arm in arm. He would hold her chair for her in the dining room.

You could sense it. It was a beautiful relationship.

BOB CASE:

There's never been a greater love affair in any sport.

I have a picture of Casey and I sitting in the backyard in the seats from the Polo Grounds that he was sitting in when he met Edna. Those were the seats where Edna was sitting with Irish Meusel's wife when he met her.

They pulled them out of the Polo Grounds, and Casey had them in his backyard by the diving board of his swimming pool. Casey valued them.

That was a great love affair. Casey was a tough guy; he used to get in brawls, get in fights. When he married Edna, he was like thirty-four years old. Edna came from a very wealthy, high-society family. She dressed in designer clothes. A beautiful lady. Classy, intelligent. She took

Casey—he was way over on one side of the spectrum, and she was way over on the other side—and she put him right in the middle. He would never do anything that would make her look bad. She put the finishing touches on the diamond. She was a major, major influence on Casey's life. He loved her so much. She polished him.

They had a great sense of humor together. They loved each other. In his den, Casey had the autographed balls from each of the ten pennant-winning teams. Edna would come in and say, "Casey, you've got to do this. Casey, you've got to do that."

He would kind of wink and look over at me and say, "Yeah, Bob. You see her autograph on the sweet spot of all those baseballs up there." The sweet spot is where the manager signs.

When she got Alzheimer's, that broke him up. I think that was the worst thing that ever happened to him.

I went up to the house one day, and I knocked on the door and the maid answered the door. I said, "Where's Casey?"

She said, "Bob, I don't know where he is, but I think he's up at the park."

So I drive my car up to the park. This must have been 1971 or '72. I drive my car up there, and I see some Little Leaguers playing baseball. Casey had an old Cadillac at that time. I see his Cadillac. I walk over and he's staring into space. Just staring. He's not even watching the game.

I said, "Casey, what's going on?"

He looked at me and he said, "She's batty."

I said, "What do you mean?"

He said, "She's batty. Bob, she can't add the checks anymore."

He tried to take care of her himself for the last couple of years. He'd dress her up, and he'd have people come in and do her hair, shower her, and everything. Then it got to be too much. I think that was his saddest day, when he had to put her in the convalescent hospital.

RON SWOBODA:

I asked him at one of these Old-Timers Games, "Casey, how's Edna?"

He said, "She's lost her mind."

They were great friends. When my first son was born, we ended up in the same restaurant with them. My oldest son was having a little trouble with colic. Edna had to take the baby, and she had the baby in the air, over her face.

I'm going, *Oh, please, not now.* My son had been spitting up pretty regularly.

He didn't.

She was an interesting lady. They were an interesting pair. They had seen so much in this world.

HARRY MINOR:

Edna was in a rest home below where Casey lived there in Glendale. I used to take him down there to see Edna. He'd wheel her around the hallways and talk to everybody with her.

BOB CASE:

When she was in that convalescent home, they took Casey's car away and he couldn't drive. That convalescent home was at least two miles from Casey's house.

Edna always loved chocolate donuts, chocolate candy. She craved chocolate. Casey would go and get this See's candy out here, and he'd walk them down to her in the convalescent home.

She didn't even recognize him. But he'd walk down every day and take these chocolate donuts and candy to her.

3. BE NICE TO THE LITTLE PEOPLE.

BOB CASE:

At the bottom of the street near his house was a Kentucky Fried Chicken. Casey would go in and get a three-piece dinner—three pieces of chicken, cole slaw. And he would give the girl a five-dollar bill.

I was always shocked. In 1970, you didn't tip five dollars when the meal was $3.95 in a fast-food joint. But he always did that kind of stuff.

Casey would always tell me, "Take care of the little guy." If there's one thing he taught me in my life, it was to take care of the cab driver, the guy that shines your shoes.

I overtip. My wife always asks, "Why do you overtip?" It's because Casey always told me to take care of the little guy. That's one of the things I loved about him.

TOM FERGUSON:

I was the visiting-clubhouse man in Milwaukee in '57. The Yankees opened the series in Milwaukee, and then we went on to New York to play the next three games. They usually give the clubhouse man a little gratuity for the two days that the team was there.

We beat them the first two games. We had the Yankees 2–0. Casey said to me, "I'm not going to pay you now. We're coming back. I'll be back and I'll take good care of you when I get back."

I said, "Okay, Case."

Sure enough, they came back to Milwaukee. He came back and paid me well.

RON HUNT:

Casey is the one who taught me that without the fans, we ain't worth shit. He showed us that by being out there, signing autographs, all the time. If this old man can be out there doing that, why shouldn't we?

The little people include the littlest people, kids. **BOB CASE,** *who grew up near Stengel:*

My grandmother played poker with Casey's wife, Edna. I used to go swimming in his pool. He had the first pool in Glendale. I used to go swimming there when I was a kid. He had avocado trees back there, and he used to always give us avocados. We had Thanksgiving together when I was a kid. He would sit down and tell us stories about

Mickey Mantle, playing against Babe Ruth. Here I was, this kid—my parents were alcoholics—and Casey took me under his wing.

Edna's sister was named Mae Hunter. She lived out in the Malibu Mountains. Her husband was George Hunter; he used to manage Hoot Gibson. George Hunter was one of Casey's best friends.

They would drive from Glendale to spring training in Florida together every year. I would go out there to Mae Hunter's every summer when I was a kid, and I would live there. Casey would come out there, and every time he would come out, he'd say, "Bobby, get your baseball." And he was an older man then—this was when he was managing the Yankees. He'd play catch with me on the front lawn for like an hour. I'd go back to school and tell my friends, "I played catch with Casey Stengel." They wouldn't believe me.

Mae Hunter and George Hunter had a son named Buddy. Casey loved Buddy. If you see any old Hoot Gibson movies, Buddy is the little kid riding on a small horse next to Hoot Gibson.

Casey idolized Buddy. He was a little left-handed hitter, and Casey took him out and made a baseball player out of him.

Buddy was a pilot during the war. They got Buddy out of the war because he was their only son. Then he was killed in '42 or '43 over the Grand Canyon in an airplane. He was filming a movie called *God is My Co-pilot*, and he was killed.

That was like a son Casey didn't have. When he was killed, that shook the hell out of Casey. He'd get tears in his eyes whenever he would tell me about Buddy Hunter.

I didn't have a lot of self-esteem when I was a kid. But

I thought, *Gee, Casey really likes me. I must be worth something after all.*

I often wonder what would have happened to me if not for him. And there isn't a day that goes by that I don't thank him for it. A lot of people said I was like a son he never had. That was the tag I had. He took me under his wing.

Casey loved children. Lefty Phillips, who managed the Angels, had a team in the winter called the Brooklyn Dodger Rookies. I was the batboy. On that team was Don Drysdale, Larry Sherry. They would come out and play at Stengel Field every Saturday and Sunday.

Casey would come out and scout them. Kids would come up and Casey would put his arm around them and talk to them. "Do you play Little League? What position do you play?" He would take a bunch of kids over and buy them ice cream. He was always doing nice stuff like that. Always. *Always.*

He had these little cards made up to give out to kids. He used to carry them in his coat pocket. He would sit down and sign a hundred of them. Let's say we were going out to a banquet. We'd go out and he'd hand them out to kids. It was a picture of him. And he'd sign it, "Casey Stengel, New York Mets, Hall of Fame."

And he'd always write, "Join the Mets."

GEORGE SULLIVAN, *Red Sox visiting-team batboy in 1949, on the day the Yankees lost a close game at Fenway Park in the thick of the pennant race:*

It was wonderful seeing these guys, as batboys, because they had absolutely nothing to gain from you—especially in the case of visiting-team batboy. They don't even have to live with me half the year. They see me a number of times a year and that's it. So you know if they're nice to you, usually it's a pretty good indicator of what kind of a person they are.

A telltale thing was after the game. The Red Sox won the game, 4–1. Now there's a week to go in the season— it's going to be a whole season in one week.

The Yankees were really down. This slide had started six, seven, eight weeks before. Finally, the Red Sox had caught them. You had to know what was going through Casey's mind: *Boy, if we blow this thing, I'll never hear the end of it. They were right; he is a clown. What is he doing managing these champions?*

I'm going about my chores. The Yankees were very quiet. Nobody was saying much of anything. Hushed tones. Casey had finished dressing and finished talking to the press. I see him out of the corner of my eye, looking all around the room. He's looking for somebody.

A short time after, I see him and he's still looking. Then he sees me.

I'm the guy he was looking for.

He comes over and he's got two one-dollar bills rolled up in his fist.

He said something like, "You done splendid, kid."

Here he is, maybe blown the pennant, maybe blown his job. Who knows? And he's worried about finding me, to give me a tip.

The weight of the world is on his shoulders, and he's worried about giving me a tip.

By the way, in those days, that was a pretty good tip.

CHUCK SYMONDS, batboy for Stengel's Oakland
Oaks:

The batboys, the clubhouse kids, we were all part of the
team. Whatever the team did, parties or whatever, we
were invited. So when we won the pennant in '48, they
gave us the ride down through the main part of Oakland.
They gave us a parade. I was in the second car, right
behind Casey. He was really hooting and hollering.

We did spring training one year down in the San
Fernando Valley. Casey lived down in Glendale. He and
his wife, Edna, had no children. They kind of took a liking to me. I stayed with them. He was kind of like my
father-away-from-home. It was a lot of laughs to live in
the same house with him. Just a jolly attitude, really. He
never looked down on anybody. Just funny little quips.
Just fun to be around. He even offered to take me to the
Yankees in '49. But I was just starting high school; I
wanted to stay home. He was just that type of person.

I traveled with them, and Casey always made sure I
had a dollar for trolley fare, or movie money. The train
trips I took with him were a lot of fun. He would play
cards with me. The fatherly thing.

I really admired the guy. He never said a cross word to
me in the three years I worked with him. He let me take
batting practice. He let me take infield.

He let me play in a spring training game one time. We
were playing the Stockton Ports. I was fourteen years old.
He let me pinch-hit.

I wasn't expecting it at all. I was up in the on-deck circle with the bats, like I always was. He just called upon
me to hit. I hit the ball to shortstop, but I forced the guy
at second base. Casey gave me a chance to do that.

GEORGE SULLIVAN:

This was sometime in August. It was a Friday night game, the opening of a series.

Jim Turner was running the pitchers in the outfield. They would gather out in left-center field, sort of near the end of the scoreboard near the flag pole, and they would run toward the right-field line. I would always ask the visiting pitching coach if they needed anybody to help shag flies before the game.

And here I am in left field. You had to watch yourself a little bit, especially with right-handed hitters spraying that area. Up steps Joe DiMaggio, and he is really raking them out there. It may be my imagination, but the balls he hit sounded differently. They had a hum. I don't know if they had a topspin or what. Here's Joe DiMaggio hitting them to my left, to my right. Right at me. I'm catching some of them.

Meanwhile, I'm watching Turner, watching the pitchers. All of a sudden, I feel this sharp pain in my lower back. It flipped me. I went ass over tea kettle. I'm looking up at the sky. It's dusk and the light towers are on.

All of a sudden, I'm surrounded by faces looking down at me—like I was lying in the middle of a football huddle, looking up. Just heads looking down at me. Joe Page. Snuffy Stirnweiss. I can still see them.

What had happened was, Turner had hit a line drive. He hadn't gotten the ball up in the air. He had gotten it about three feet up in the air and it hit the base of my spine. It just numbed me.

They're all saying, "Don't move. We'll get a stretcher."

I ignored what the Yankees were saying and I popped

right up. I was bewildered a little bit by it. I went running off the field by the third-base dugout.

Casey was the only one in the dugout. He had one foot on the floor of the dugout and his other foot was on the second step. He was looking out at the direction I was coming in from. And I was embarrassed.

So I veered to his right a little bit and came in a little further up in the dugout.

And as I passed, he said, "Where did it get you, kid? In the ass?"

I said, "No, Case, in my back."

He said, "Go in and have Gus give you a rub."

I said, "No, no, no. Thank you. I'm fine."

All these things point to the kind of guy he was. A lot of guys would have ignored you.

4. EAT, DRINK, AND BE MERRY.
Last call will come soon enough.

JACK LANG:

What did he drink? You name it. I would see him go from an Old Fashioned to a scotch and soda to a martini. He could drink four or five different drinks at the bar. Mostly he wanted Old Fashioneds. Whatever you put in front of him, he would drink.

He didn't want any of the players to drink at the hotel bars. That was one of his big rules. He said, "That's *my* bar. You guys stay out of there. There are enough other bars for you."

He always had a funny line. He loved to just sit at the bar and talk to people. No matter who it was, he'd strike up a conversation. It was one of the ways he learned as much as he did. He loved to talk to anybody.

EDDIE JOOST:

He and Frankie Frisch were great friends. They were drinking buddies.

There was the hotel on Bay State Road. I lived there; a lot of the guys did. They had a place on the roof for dancing and dinner.

Every time Pittsburgh came in, Frankie Frisch and Stengel would get so loaded, they'd be throwing glasses around.

Every once in a while, they'd throw them out. "That's all! You two, get out!"

TOMMY HOLMES:

He showed me something when we were playing Pittsburgh, Frankie Frisch's team. They played together with the Giants.

We scored a whole lot of runs against them after there were two out in the ninth inning. We're still down by two runs.

He said, "I can't gamble on getting any more hits. I need a home run."

He said, "Chet! Chet Ross!" Chet Ross was one of our outfielders at the time. I don't know who Chet hit for, but whoever it was, he was furious.

Believe it or not, Chet hits a home run. We win.

Frankie Frisch hollers over, "You Dutch bastard!"

Casey says, "I'll see you over at the Kenmore. We'll have a couple of drinks."

HANK BAUER:

He drank a lot. Manhattans. He'd have press conferences at two or three o'clock in the morning.

DARIO LODIGIANI:

Sometimes he would go out and have those two- or three-martini lunches. Then he would show up at the ballpark, and he would coach at first base instead of third base. He said when he was coaching at third base, he couldn't see the ball very well.

MAURY ALLEN:

There was a time in 1964 in Saint Louis. There was a nightclub we were staying at, in the Chase Hotel.

We all went to dinner at the nightclub. After the dinner was over, which was maybe twelve, one o'clock in the morning, we adjourned to the bar. And as the night goes on, more and more guys leave. It's two-thirty, three in the morning, and I'm at the bar alone with Casey Stengel, and he's telling these stories. You know—"Zack Wheat was the greatest outfielder I ever played with," and "Ty Cobb was this"—all about these players in the '20s and '30s. Which I found fascinating.

I'm twenty-nine and he's seventy-four. And I'm running

out of steam but he's not. Finally, when they closed the bar at four o'clock in the morning, the guy says, "Last call."

Casey says, "Give me two scotches." I get a beer and we sit there.

Now it's maybe five o'clock in the morning. We're sitting at the bar and he's still talking. Finally, I realize I'm going to fall off the chair. I'm gonna die. I've got to go up to my room.

I say, "Casey, I've gotta go. I'm exhausted."

So I get up and I start walking out the door, and he says to me, "If you're down for breakfast at seven o'clock, I'll buy."

So what I did was, I went up to my room and I said, "I'm going to get him this time, and then I'm going to write a story about it—that he was bullshitting me."

So I go up to my room and I laid down for about an hour. I set the alarm clock and I get up at seven o'clock and I come downstairs.

And there's Casey Stengel standing in front of a potted palm in the hotel lobby. He's leaning against the potted palm at a quarter after seven. And I come down and I still look like I'm dead.

He says, "Okay, kid, let's go have breakfast!"

He was as chipper as could be.

5. BE LOYAL.

BOB CASE:

He kept in contact with a lot of the old guys. I was fortunate to meet all these guys. Charlie Deal was a good friend of Casey's. He was the last surviving member of the 1914

Boston Braves. He was the third baseman. Wilbur Cooper was out here; he'd come by to see Casey. Babe Herman was his neighbor.

We went out and saw Chief Meyers. He was the catcher with the Giants; he was Christy Mathewson's catcher. He was an Indian and he lived in a trailer.

He loved Ernie Lombardi. Casey and I went up to the World Series in '73. We went and saw Lombardi. He was working in a gas station. Casey was upset by that.

Dutch Zwilling was his best friend. He's the last name listed in the Baseball Encyclopedia. They played against each other in high school. His wife was Casey's girlfriend in high school. Dutch later scouted for the Mets. Dutch played for all three Chicago teams—the Cubs, the White Sox, and the Chicago Whales of the Federal League. He was a little guy, like 5–6.

He was over all the time. All through the Sixties and Seventies, Dutch was with Casey all the time. They would go out and scout baseball together. He would run around with Dutch. Both of them were horrible drivers. Casey's cars had dents in them all the time. He'd back into things. He could go out and drink pretty heavy and drive like a maniac.

When George Weiss died, that shook him up. When Frankie Frisch died, he cried. When George Weiss died, he cried. A lot of other people died, but I don't think that it affected him like those two.

———◆———

Stengel's magnificent rapport with newspapermen wasn't just for the sake of slick public relations. Mostly, Casey was good to them because they were his friends. **ART JOHNSON:**

He was a great man to interview, as far as reporters were concerned. They used to come into the dugout every day and interview him and talk to him. They'd sit on the bench for hours. He'd tell them anything they wanted— or tell them things they didn't want to hear.

They had great times with him.

Maury Allen:

This is 1962. I'm a young reporter covering the new New York Mets. This is the middle of June of their first season. We've gone to spring training and the team is organized. A terrible team. Every time they win, it's like winning the World Series.

One day in June, I said to Casey, "I want to do a big profile feature on you." He said, "All right, get out to the ballpark at three o'clock."

This was at the Polo Grounds, where in those days they played eight o'clock night games. I'm a young reporter. I get to the ballpark at two o'clock and I walk out onto the field. There's one person in uniform on the field, and it's Casey Stengel sitting in the dugout. Nobody else is there.

I go over and we start talking. We go on to about four o'clock. From two o'clock to four o'clock, he's doing a monologue on his whole life. And he's only up to about 1922 by this time.

The Polo Grounds clubhouse was in center field. As we're talking, coming across the field I see a TV camera and about four or five people coming across. As they get closer, I recognize that's it's a very big New York television journalist by the name of Gabe Pressman.

He walks up to Casey Stengel—this is at four o'clock, two hours after we started—and he looks at Stengel and he says, "Oh, Casey. Remember we had an interview scheduled?"

AP/WIDE WORLD PHOTO

On September 18, 1963, Casey and Edna say goodbye to the Polo Grounds, home to Stengel's hapless Mets their first three seasons. The team would take up residence at the new Shea Stadium the following spring.

Casey continues to talk to me. He suddenly looks up at Gabe Pressman and in a very abrasive voice, he says to Gabe Pressman, "Don't you see I'm busy talking to my writers?"

Not *writer*, but *writers*. And I was the only person he was talking to.

The point of the whole story is that he was incredibly loyal to the everyday working sportswriters—the guys who covered the club and who were there every day, listened to him every day, spent time with him at the hotel bars, and hung around and listened to his stories.

He was incredibly sort of devoted to us. He looked at television, radio, magazine guys, and anybody else as sort of outsiders.

ROD KANEHL:

I think he had an agreement with the newspapermen. They could write how terrible the Mets were, but they couldn't write how terrible individual players were. And they didn't. They didn't write about individuals.

Cosell and Branca had a five-minute pregame and a five-minute postgame show in '62, on radio. Howard and Casey hated each other.

Tim Harkness got on the Howard Cosell show, and Howard would do the best he could to get someone to say something bad about Casey. He got Harkness to agree that Casey was asleep on the bench. And Harkness was gone.

Cosell and I were good friends. Howard would have me on the show all the time, and he would present me questions about Stengel. And I would duck them. We'd get off the show and Cosell would say, "Well, you did it again. You saved your job." Casey and Howard hated each other.

BOB SALES:

He had different birthdays in the press guide and in the baseball register and other places. You'd ask him and he'd say, "Well, you guys always want exclusives."

He would come to us and say, "I know you've got to write a story because you've got a night game. I figured I'll let you know that I'm going to play Johnny Lewis against a lefty." Things like that. He'd give us an easy first-edition story.

He could make your job very easy because he was very seductive. You'd always go to Casey.

JACK LANG:

He was fabulous with the writers. He couldn't stand the microphone guys. He'd chase Howard Cosell out of the dugout. He didn't like Howard Cosell. That's why Cosell carried on a feud with him for the rest of his life.

It was so typical of him. When a guy would come around during the World Series with a microphone wanting to ask him a question, Casey would say, "Where were you in the middle of August? All my writers were with me all year."

In those days, the writers would always be the same guys. I remember I covered the Brooklyn Dodgers from 1946 to 1957. And pretty much the same guys who were covering the team in '46 were covering them when they left town in '57, except for one or two papers that had folded.

He cherished the writers; they were with him all year. And they would be at the bar with him at night and see him at breakfast in the morning.

The day he got fired—the Yankees say he resigned, but there are reports all around that he was fired—I was sitting in back of him at the time.

The Yankees had announced that he resigned.

Somebody said, "The AP says you were fired."

Casey said, "What does the UP say?"

He was a savvy guy. He knew what was going on at all times.

He was so aware of the newspaperman's job. There was an incident one year when I was covering the Yankees. It was in Saint Petersburg. We played games at one o'clock in the afternoon at Al Lang Field in Saint Petersburg. Two blocks away was the hotel where the club stayed. After the game, they had a little hospitality suite for the writers to come up and have a drink with Casey and club officials and other people.

I remember going over after a game one afternoon, and we're sitting there and we're drinking with Casey. The morning guys, Trimble, John Drebinger, people like that, after they wrote their stories in the press box, they would come over to the hotel and have a couple of drinks.

After a while, one by one, all the morning guys had left the room. Casey realized that the only ones left in the room were afternoon writers. They hadn't written their stories yet.

He said, "I know you guys can't write the box score. So I'll tell you what I'm going to do tomorrow."

He knew that we had to have second-day stories. He was aware of that. He knew that our job was to come up with something different from what had appeared in the morning papers.

The next best thing to a New York newspaperman was an out-of-town newspaperman. **DICK FENLON** *of the* Columbus Dispatch:

I talked to him one-on-one only once. It was at an Old-Timers Game in Cincinnati after he'd stopped managing. He wore a Yankees uniform, even though he had last managed the expansion Mets. After the introductions, he retired to the clubhouse. I found him there sitting in front of a locker, pulling off his socks. He looked up and, without an introduction, began talking as if he had known me all his life.[1]

Even if they were from way out of town. Just as long as they were newspapermen. **TOMMY BYRNE:**

We went around the world in '55. We went over in Japan

and played twenty-eight games. We played twenty-eight games in thirty days, or something like that.

He got along great with the Japanese press over there. I didn't think he knew much Japanese, but he made out like he did.

Newspapermen were his friends. GEORGE VECSEY of The New York Times:

I remember one visit to the coast around 1968, when Casey entertained us at his bank, where I felt compelled to open an account.

Five years later, Casey came up to me in the crowded World Series press room and stuck one of those powerful forefingers into my chest and barked, "You still got money in my bank!"[2]

JACK LANG:

We were out in California and he came to a game one night at Dodger Stadium. Leonard Koppett, who was then with *The Times*, said to me, "Let's go down and sit with the old man."

We went down in the second or third inning. We sat with him for a couple of innings behind the Mets dugout and had a lot of fun talking to him and reminiscing.

Shortly thereafter, he died. It was the last time I saw him alive.

He was probably the most unforgettable character I ever met. I treasure the fact that I had six, seven years with him. He was just a delightful person to be around.

6. Stay open to new friends.

There are no strangers. . . .

———◆———

Bob Case:

Casey loved people. Genuinely loved people. I never saw him stiff anybody for an autograph. I never saw him stiff anybody for anything. He would sit and talk baseball all night long. He loved Edna, number one. Then he loved baseball.

He was the best ambassador for baseball. And I mean a real ambassador, not a phony ambassador. He treated everybody the same. He would treat a president of the United States the same as he would a shoeshine boy.

We used to stay at the Essex House in New York. He'd talk to the cab drivers, he'd talk to the shoeshine boys. If you liked baseball, you were his friend. To me, that's what an ambassador was. He was beautiful to everybody.

———◆———

Harry Minor:

I couldn't scout and stay close to him, because he would draw such a crowd. I'd just drop him and go to work.

We used to have a high school tournament out here in Balboa Park. Four diamonds, with games going on all at once.

Casey would sit on a trash can, and there would be thirty people around him. All the time.

———◆———

BOB CASE:

Nobody attracted people like Casey. He was almost like the Pied Piper. You'd walk in somewhere—and he had kind of a loud voice—and people would come to him. It would just kill you.

Women would love to kiss him. He would have lipstick all over him. Good-looking, young women liked to kiss Casey. There was something about him. They just had to kiss him.

One time I was up in Lake Tahoe. It was about 1968. I was at my ex-wife's picnic. She was in real estate. There were about a hundred people there and they were playing a game of softball.

She says to me, "Bob, there's a guy over there who says he played ball with Casey Stengel."

I said, "No kidding?" So I went over and there was this little guy who must have been seventy-five, eighty years old.

He said, "Oh, yeah. I played with Casey back with the Brooklyn Dodgers."

He said his name.

I said, "I'll be glad to give Casey the message."

So I got home and I see Casey. I was always running into his ex-teammates. I said, "Casey, I ran into one of your old teammates over the weekend up in Lake Tahoe."

He said, "Who's that?"

I told him the guy's name.

And he just stopped. Like he saw a ghost.

I said, "What's wrong?"

He told me that this guy was like one of the head guys in the Irish mafia in Saint Louis. He played with the Dodgers in the teens. Casey told me the guy wore silk hats, silk suits. He said, "And when we'd go into Saint Louis, he'd take us to all night places. He knew everybody."

Casey knew everybody, everywhere.

GEORGE VECSEY, writing in The New York Times:

It was well after midnight in a tavern in Milwaukee. Casey Stengel and his Greek chorus of journalists were tackling huge platters of fried potatoes and sausages, and steins of beer.

Casey was telling us how, twenty years earlier, he managed the minor-league team in Milwaukee. He was describing a tornado that he said had blown him clear across the street in 1944. He stood up from the table and did a ballet imitation of flying through the air. He looked like Peter Pan with elephant ears.

Those of us who had gone light on the beer were aware of a pack of motorcycle people sitting at the bar. At least in my mind, there was some undertone of menace as those men of tattoos and axle grease sat gaping at the Old Man.

But Casey fixed that. He bridged the gap between the sport jacket crowd and the black leather jacket crowd by including the motorcycle gang in his Socratic dialogue about whether the Mets should acquire Roy McMillan, an aging shortstop.

"Now, you want to give me McMillan, who is thirty-three and we don't know if he can throw. Then who do you want, Hook? Hook won a lot of games for me and he has a lovely family. Edna says I can't trade him. Would you like to talk to Edna for me?"

Charmed by being included in this bit of baseball gossip, the leather jacket crowd relaxed and crunched on their beer cans in peace. Casey had made this world a little safer for the Mets and their entourage.[3]

GEORGE SULLIVAN, the Fenway Park batboy who went on to cover the team for the **Boston Herald-Traveler:**

It wasn't too many years later that I was back covering the Red Sox. Stengel, he always remembered. He always went out of his way to be helpful.

One day I was over there doing a sidebar, and Casey and I were talking before a game. I don't remember how the conversation came up, but my father's name came into it. My father was a great Casey Stengel fan. My father was a great baseball fan, but he particularly liked Stengel. I remember hearing Casey Stengel stories for a long time.

I said something about the fact that my father was always a great fan of his.

Casey said, "Bring him in! Bring him in!"

I said something to the effect of, "That's all right, you don't have to do that. . . ."

I thought he was just being nice.

He said, "No! I'd love talking to him." I thought he was just being nice, but he really insisted about it.

He said, "Bring him in tomorrow! Bring him in before the game tomorrow! I'd love to talk with him."

So I called up my father and said, "Let's go to the game tomorrow."

I think this was in '59. This was another moment when he should have been in a real bad mood. Under pressure. It was like a five-game series and the Red Sox swept them. And that was not a great Red Sox team. To sweep the Yankees at Fenway was really something. And this was in the midst of that series. Casey had every reason to be in not too good a humor.

Before the game, the writers would be sitting on the stairs and he'd be regaling them with stories. So my father came in during batting practice. Here's Casey talking to the writers. They were sitting on the steps like they were in school. I can still see them.

My father and I come out of that gate by the third-base dugout and we come around the corner. I was going to have my father sit by the bat rack until Casey wanted to come down and talk.

Casey sees us immediately. He says, "Well, gentlemen, there's a very important person I have to see right now. I'm going to have to cut this off right here."

He made his exit from the writers and he came down and I introduced them. And that's all I had to do. Casey took over and the two of them hit it off instantly. Once I could see that it was instant chemistry there, I sort of eased off and joined the writers, who were sitting on their hands now. They were all figuring my father was an old-time ballplayer or something. My father, with his straw hat on. They're sitting down by the bat rack and they're talking.

I'm just making sure everything is okay. I'm still keeping an eye on them. I hear Casey say, "You're full of shit, and I'll tell you why . . ."

That's when I relaxed. I knew my father was fully accepted, because Casey only said that to people he liked.

My father was just thrilled. I purposely took the day off. And so my father and I sat in the stands and watched the game together. My father wasn't in the best of health in his later years. It was the only Red Sox game, the only ball game, my father and I ever went to together.

After the game, I went down and I thanked Casey. He said, "No, I should be thanking you."

7. BE GENEROUS.

With your money, with your time, with everything.

RUGGER ARDIZOIA, right-handed pitcher for Stengel's 1946 Oakland Oaks:

Every time we won a ball game, Casey would get two cases of beer. He'd buy it out of his own pocket. You'd be sitting in a hotel restaurant, and he'd come by and sit with you and he'd pick up the check.

We would play down in Hollywood. Casey lived in Glendale, the next town north of L.A.

At the ballpark, he'd get enough cabs to take everybody up to his house. His wife would be there, with other people. They had been barbecuing the whole time. He had a huge, beautiful home, with a huge garden. That's where we would stay out at night.

When you walked in, he gave you half a pint of whatever you drank, a bottle of beer, whatever you wanted. You'd sit there a while and talk and have hors d'oeuvres. And then they'd feed you this barbecue.

And when it was all over, he'd have the cabs take us down to Hollywood to catch the train back to Oakland that night. He'd pay for all that.

DARIO LODIGIANI, *who played infield for Stengel's Oaks:*

Casey was a good-hearted son of a gun. When he had to let a ballplayer go, he'd give them a few hundred dollars and say, "Go buy yourself something." He was a soft-hearted guy that way.

In the '48 season, we were getting into an important series and he wanted to win it.

He said, "If you win tonight, I'll buy you all a five-dollar steak dinner."

And at the end of the season, we had a two-game lead. We were playing a doubleheader. San Francisco was in second place. We were two games out in front.

We win one game or the Seals lose a ball game, we win the pennant. He said, "You win the first game today and I'll buy you all a five-dollar steak dinner."

We went out and won the game. Sure enough, he gave us all five bucks apiece. That was a lot of money in them days. He had plenty, you know.

MEL DUEZABOU, *Oaks outfielder:*

I do remember we had won a couple of games in a row. He said, "You guys win this next one and it will be a five-dollar steak dinner for you guys."

We'd win the game and the trainer would stand by the clubhouse door. And as each guy went out, he would hand us five bucks.

In those days, five dollars was a helluva lot of money, and it would get you a helluva steak dinner.

BOB CASE:

He was generous. It was hard to pick up a tab around Casey. He was giving and good-hearted. He paid for the funerals of a lot of old ballplayers. People don't realize that.

Two years into retirement in 1967, Casey poses with business manager and friend Bob Case near Stengel's backyard pool in Glendale, California. They are seated in the Polo Grounds chairs in which Casey met his wife, Edna, four decades earlier.

CHUCK STEVENS:

He was probably one of the nicest men I ever met, particularly later on, when I became secretary of the ballplayers association. He was a very caring man, for all of the old-timers.

Casey later on became a very well-to-do man. So he was in position to do some nice things. And he did.

I don't think he ever forgot that there were guys who were not as fortunate as he was.

The association had an annual dinner. There would be four or five hundred people there. We held this in Los Angeles. Case would always come to the dinner, no matter what was going on. If he'd been in the World Series or whatever, he'd always be there. He'd always be at the head table, because Casey was the director for many years. He was popular.

So he'd come to this meeting and he was always the speaker. Casey would begin to speak, and we never knew how long he was going to go on. He had the reputation for cleaning the hall out a time or two.

So when I became the secretary, I would always arrange the seating so I would be seated next to Case. And when he got on the microphone, he would be within arm's reach.

I emceed the event, and I would introduce Case and he would take off and I would have my watch handy. I'd give him an appropriate amount of time, and then I would start to tug his coattails.

He'd be talking and swinging at my hand to get it off his coattails. He called me "Stevie." He'd be whispering to me, "Okay, Stevie. Okay, Stevie."

This went on year after year after year.

I'll tell you how caring he was. He was an old, old man at this time. Everybody knew he was old and he was beginning to slow up. We all began to protect him a little bit, to be sure that we didn't overtax him.

There was a banquet in central California. There was a Hall of Famer who was supposed to be the speaker there. I won't use any names. At the last moment, the Hall of Famer stood the people up.

Harry Minor, who for many years scouted for the Mets, was called. He knew Casey well. He called Casey in Glendale and wanted to know if he would come up and substitute for the Hall of Famer. I'm guessing this is, minimum, a 250-, 275-mile trip.

Casey said, "Sure. How quick can you pick me up?"

I've got to say he was eighty-two or eighty-three at the time. What I'm saying, it was not an easy chore for a fellow of that age.

Harry Minor picked him up and brought him up, and Casey just stopped the house. He was gracious to do that, for people he didn't even really know. The people there talked about that for years. He was like that.

※

HARRY MINOR:

Another guy was supposed to be there, but he didn't show up. Willie Mays. Casey got the call to fill in.

Driving up Route 99 with Casey in the car, he's such a recognizable guy that people would see him and start honking the horn. He had that craggly face that you couldn't mistake.

When you drove Casey, you never said a word. He'd talk the whole time. You'd try to get a word in edgewise, he'd just ramble on. He was great. The trip would go in a hurry. He'd get mad at you if you missed a turn, though.

I have a friend who's a deputy sheriff down in Bakersfield. I always stop and see him when I'm near there. So Casey and I are driving back, and I said, "Casey, I've got to stop and call my friend here. I can't go through Bakersfield without at least calling to say hello."

Casey says, "Well, let's go see him! Get a drink!"

So I knock on my friend's door. He was an ex-baseball player. And here's Casey Stengel standing there with me. My friend just about fell over.

We come in and we sat around and talked, had a drink. Next thing you know, my friend disappeared. And here he comes with the whole neighborhood. They all came in and Casey just ate it up. He loved it. He signed autographs for an hour.

Casey was that way. You know, at Dodger Stadium, he

would draw such a crowd. They would hold them back. As soon as the inning ended, they would let five or six people come down. He would sit there and sign autographs all night.

8. BE YOURSELF, ALL THE WAY TO THE END.

BOB CASE:

Casey had this big bump on his stomach. He had had an operation, and there was a scar down the middle of his stomach. And in the middle of this scar was a bump. He used to show it to me. I thought it was like a hernia.

Rod Dedeaux sent him to a doctor. They saw it was cancer and they went in to take it out. They saw it was inoperable. They sewed him back up and he died a little while later.

I saw him at the hospital the day before he died. The Pirates were playing the Dodgers and the game was on the TV. Casey got up out of the hospital bed and he stood up during the national anthem.

The next day, a woman who Casey brought in to work for him, June Bowlin, was there. She said he stood up during the national anthem and said, "I might as well stand up. This may be the last time."

HARRY MINOR:

Where Casey lived, there's a little graveyard. That's where all of Edna's family is buried. Casey was fighting with Edna's family. They had some disagreements.

He never called me Harry. He always called me Minor. He said, "Minor, if you let them bury me down there in that cemetery, I'll come back and haunt you for the rest of your life."

So when we started planning (his funeral), I told Rod Dedeaux, "Don't you dare put him in there. I don't want Casey haunting me."

So we get him in Forest Lawn up there in Glendale. Casey and Edna are there. There's a nice monument, with one of his quotes: "There comes a time in every man's life, and I've had plenty of them."

BOB CASE:

In his casket, we buried him with his Yankees uniform and his Mets uniform. We had his '62 Mets home shirt and pants and hat. And we had his '60 road Yankees shirt, hat, and pants.

And he had the cleats. And a picture of Edna.

CASEY STENGEL'S YEAR-BY-YEAR MANAGERIAL RECORD

Year	League	Team	Games	W	L	Pct	Finish
1934	NL	Brooklyn	153	71	81	.467	6th in NL
1935	NL	Brooklyn	154	70	83	.458	5th in NL
1936	NL	Brooklyn	156	67	87	.435	7th in NL
1938	NL	Boston Braves	153	77	75	.507	5th in NL
1939	NL	Boston Braves	152	63	88	.417	7th in NL
1940	NL	Boston Braves	152	65	87	.428	7th in NL
1941	NL	Boston Braves	156	62	92	.403	7th in NL
1942	NL	Boston Braves	150	59	89	.399	7th in NL
1943	NL	Boston Braves	107	47	60	.439	6th in NL
1949	AL	N.Y. Yankees	155	97	57	.630	Won World Series
1950	AL	N.Y. Yankees	155	98	56	.636	Won World Series
1951	AL	N.Y. Yankees	154	98	56	.636	Won World Series

Year	League	Team	Games	W	L	Pct	Finish
1952	AL	N.Y. Yankees	154	95	59	.617	Won World Series
1953	AL	N.Y. Yankees	151	99	52	.656	Won World Series
1954	AL	N.Y. Yankees	155	103	51	.669	2nd in AL
1955	AL	N.Y. Yankees	154	96	58	.623	Won AL Pennant
1956	AL	N.Y. Yankees	154	97	57	.630	Won World Series
1957	AL	N.Y. Yankees	154	98	56	.636	Won AL Pennant
1958	AL	N.Y. Yankees	155	92	62	.597	Won World Series
1959	AL	N.Y. Yankees	155	79	75	.513	3rd in AL
1960	AL	N.Y. Yankees	155	97	57	.630	Won AL Pennant
1962	NL	N.Y. Mets	161	40	120	.250	10th in NL
1963	NL	N.Y. Mets	162	51	111	.315	10th in NL
1964	NL	N.Y. Mets	163	53	109	.327	10th in NL
1965	NL	N.Y. Mets	96	31	64	.326	10th in NL
Grand Total			**3766**	**1905**	**1842**	**.508**	

Total by Team

Brooklyn Dodgers	**463**	**208**	**251**	**.453**
Boston Braves	**870**	**373**	**491**	**.432**
New York Yankees	**1851**	**1149**	**696**	**.623**
New York Mets	**582**	**175**	**404**	**.302**

NOTES

Chapter 1: The Old Professor
1. *Houston Chronicle*, May 4, 1992.
2. *Boston Globe*, Sept. 5, 1965.
3. *St. Louis Post-Dispatch*, July 8, 1990.

Chapter 2: Students, Good and Bad
1. *The New York Times*, Aug. 31, 1965.
2. *The Saturday Evening Post*, July 31, 1965.
3. New York Journal-American, May 23, 1963.
4. *The New York Times*, Aug. 31, 1965.

Chapter 3: Class Clowns
1. *Reader's Digest*, October 1967.

Chapter 4: Selected Lectures
1. *Washington Post*, March 11, 1959.
2 *The New York Times*, Sept. 20, 1981.
3. *Boston Herald*, May 11, 1960.
4. *Boston Herald*, April 18, 1964.
5. *Boston Herald*, Oct. 2, 1960.
6. *Boston Globe*, July 28, 1966.
7. David Cataneo, *Peanuts and Crackerjack*

(Nashville: Rutledge Hill Press, 1991), p. 259.

8. *Boston Globe*, July 19, 1968.

9. *Christian Science Monitor*, April 18, 1967.

10. *New York Journal-American*, May 21, 1963.

11. *Boston Herald*, March 1, 1959.

12. *New York Journal-American*, May 20, 1963.

13. *New York Journal-American*, May 20, 1963.

14. *Boston Herald*, May 8, 1949.

15. *Boston Herald*, Sept. 5, 1965.

16. *Boston Herald*, Sept. 5, 1965.

17. *New York Journal-American*, May 22, 1963.

18. Paul Dickson, *Baseball's Greatest Quotations* (New York: HarperCollins, 1991), p. 422.

19. *New York Journal-American*, May 23, 1963.

20. *New York Journal-American*, May 21, 1963.

21. *Boston Herald*, March 1, 1959.

22. *Boston Traveler*, Oct. 9, 1956.

23. David Cataneo, *Peanuts and Crackerjack*

(Nashville: Rutledge Hill Press, 1991), pp. 72–73.

24. *Boston Herald*, July 26, 1970.

25. *Boston Herald*, Dec. 9, 1952.

26. *Boston Record*, August 21, 1954.

27. *Boston Herald*, March 1, 1959.

28. *Boston Record*, Sept. 23, 1962.

29. *New York Journal-American*, May 24, 1963.

30. *New York Post*, Aug. 2, 1964.

31. *The Saturday Evening Post*, July 31, 1965.

32. *Boston Globe*, Oct. 1, 1975.

33. *Boston Globe*, Oct. 1, 1975.

34. *The New York Times*, Oct. 25, 1970.

35. *Boston Record*, March 5, 1965.

36. *Boston Herald*, April 18, 1964.

37. *Boston Herald*, Oct. 26, 1956.

38. *Boston Herald*, March 23, 1958.

39. *Boston Herald*, April 23, 1959.

40. *Christian Science Monitor*, Oct. 13, 1971.

Chapter 5: Teacher Evaluations

1. *The New York Times*, July 10, 1992.
2. *St. Petersburg Times*, Feb. 24, 1994.
3. Ira Berkow, Jim Kaplan, *The Gospel According to Casey* (New York: St. Martin's Press, 1992), p. 138.
4. Robert W. Creamer, *Stengel, His Life and Times* (New York: Simon and Schuster, 1984), p. 283.
5. *The New York Times*, Oct. 1, 1975.
6. *The Saturday Evening Post*, July 31, 1965.
7. *Boston Record*, June 19, 1942.

Chapter 6: Tuesdays with Casey

1. *Columbus Dispatch*, March 5, 1992.
2. *The New York Times*, Sept. 24, 1981.
3. *The New York Times*, Sept. 24, 1981.

BIBLIOGRAPHY

Ira Berkow and Jim Kaplan, *The Gospel According to Casey* (New York: St. Martin's Press), 1991.

David Cataneo, *Peanuts and Crackerjack* (Nashville: Rutledge Hill Press), 1991.

Robert W. Creamer, *Stengel: His Life and Times* (New York: Simon and Schuster) 1984.

Paul Dickson, *Baseball's Greatest Quotations* (New York: HarperCollins), 1991.

Frank Graham, *Casey Stengel: His Half-century in Baseball* (New York: The John Day Company), 1958.

INDEX